GETTING BEYOND THE DAY™

YOUR GUIDE TO
SURVIVING A
JOB LAYOFF

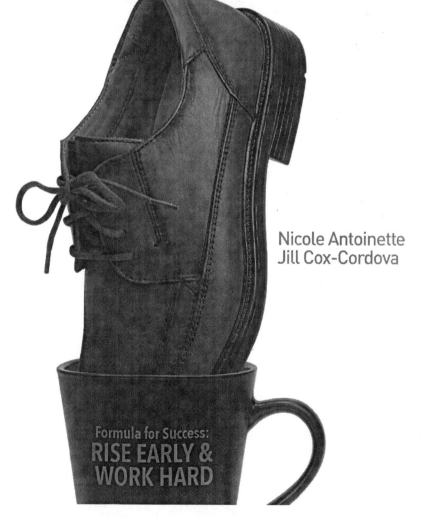

Nicole Antoinette
Jill Cox-Cordova

Formula for Success:
**RISE EARLY &
WORK HARD**

First published by Getting Beyond the Day™

ISBN 978-0-9860159-2-2

Printed in the United States of America

This book is printed on acid-free paper.

Cover designed by Neon Alfred
neonalfred.com

Getting Beyond the Day™
3255 Lawrenceville-Suwanee Rd.
Suite P250
Suwanee, GA 30024
info@gettingbeyondtheday.com
gettingbeyondtheday.com

Ordering Information:
Quantity sales. Special discounts are available on quantity purchases by corporations, associations, and others. For details, contact the publisher at the address above.

Orders by U.S. trade bookstores and wholesalers. Please contact Ingram Book Company: Tel: (800) 937-8000; Email: orders@ingrambook.com or visit ipage.ingrambook.com.

Disclaimer
The purpose of this book is to empower, educate, and offer hope. The authors of the book achieved that through their own experiences, expertise, and research. Consequently, this book should only be used as a road map. This book is not intended to be nor is it represented as legal advice. The authors are not liable or responsible, to any person, or entity, for any and all claims, demands, damages, causes of action, suits in equity of whatever kind or nature, caused or alleged to have been caused, directly or indirectly, by the information contained in this book or the authors' past or future negligence or wrongful acts.

You cannot take more out of life than what you put in!

Arthurism

Fight another Fight to Dream another Dream

DEDICATION

We dedicate this book to the millions of people
who experienced a job layoff and dared
to fight another fight to dream another dream.

Fight another Fight to Dream another Dream

ACKNOWLEDGEMENTS

We did not write this book without help. Thanks to all of our contributors, specifically Anita Rochelle Paul, Michael N. Henderson, Katherine Dorsett Bennett, and LaTrina White. We love you for understanding and capturing our vision to its fullest.

Sim Wong, you are incredibly gifted and one of the nation's best innovative minds.

Bridgett Joyce, thanks for working your magic on the interior of the book. No one else can do it better.

Gloria Spencer, thank you for editing our book to make sure it was ready for publishing.

Finally, but not least, we would also like to thank our respective families and friends—Joshan, Tony, Erica, and Phyllis (Mom), Yvette, and Donella for their love, support and patience as we wrote furiously to the finish line.

Fight another Fight to Dream another Dream

GETTING BEYOND THE DAY

BY NICOLE ANTOINETTE

The morning after the storm
Is like no other day
In that moment of time

Dreams become scattered pieces
Hopes become puddles of rain
I know I have to move on

I have to fight another fight
To dream another dream
I am getting beyond the day

Where is the reverse
Where is my recourse
So many questions

My emotions run and collide
I am left with a feeling of emptiness
Until I reach a point

I have to fight another fight
To dream another dream
I am getting beyond the day

The pain is unbearable
The shame is unimaginable
The guilt is unthinkable

I know time will make it better
But, when time stands still
And, my body is motionless

I have to fight another fight
To dream another dream
I am getting beyond the day

It is time to reflect
Time to resolve
Time to move on

Until, I am beyond the day

 *Fight another Fight to Dream another Dream*

PREFACE

Preparedness.

You think of that word as it relates to hurricanes and storms. "Make sure you are prepared for the latest disaster," the meteorologist always warns.

As the weatherperson informs us about the storm our minds start to develop a strategy to make it through. Then our thoughts shift to what to do after the storm. We begin to pull out candles, lighters, flashlights, and take inventory of food and water. We instantly kick into "survival" mode in hopes of making it through the emergency and beyond.

With technology today, storms often can be predictable. No one can predict the actual damage a storm can cause, but based upon experiences and history, we can prepare.

Unlike a meteorologist, most companies do not warn employees of the looming landfall of "Hurricane Layoff" or "Tropical Storm Downsizing." Nevertheless, even if you are warned, how do you prepare? What do you do? How do you know what to expect? Who warns you to have a plan to pay for necessities, request a severance for your next job, and have your networking contacts on standby when you are sitting comfortably in your cubicle or office one minute and a storm called a "layoff," "downsizing," or whatever term they use crashes into your reality the next?

Right. You are left with the aftermath with no equivalent of a FEMA to call.

Or, so you think.

Preparedness. That is what inspired us to write an interactive map that will guide you through today, tomorrow, and the next day. No casualties here, because you will survive this temporary setback. You must, because you chose to work again.

Our interviews with experts, countless hours of research, and our own experiences as individuals who have gone through multiple layoffs (Nicole Antoinette) and survived one (Jill Cox-Cordova) yielded what you are reading today.

You will learn how this book is customized for you and your situation, whether it is difficulty knowing where to start with your job search, your emotions, your mortgage, rent or financial assistance. This book is about *Getting Beyond the Day*™.

Fight another Fight to Dream another Dream

INTRODUCTION

When I got the news of my first job layoff, an unnatural sensation overtook me, a feeling that is hard to explain and harder to forget. It was an instant jolt like an out-of-body experience that left me feeling nervous, anxious, confused, embarrassed, and at a loss for words. It felt like I was present, yet absent. It was as if I was watching a movie scene with music playing in the background. I thought, "Is this real? Am I dreaming?" After the initial shock left me and I realized the scenario was actually happening, it felt as if my soul wanted to jump out of my skin and run, but I could not move. Then a trembling sensation came over my whole body. As I left the office, I was trying to hold onto my dignity as best I could. I hoped no one could see me shaking.

Even when I experienced my second and third layoffs, the same responses occurred. Thinking back on those experiences, I have to admit the same feelings and sensations would probably always be my natural reactions to that situation. But what I do after leaving the office does not have to be the same debilitating confusion.

With each of those three experiences I had a feeling ahead of time that I was going to be laid off. Even though they were at different times and at different companies, all three managers gave me the biggest "hint" when they told me to give my work to other people. Therefore, I trained my replacements. If that is not writing on the wall, I do not know what is.

My first job layoff occurred in 2003 when there were more information technology jobs than people to do them. Back then, if you posted an inquiry on a job search website you would have at least 25-50 messages from recruiters on your answering machine the same night. Since I felt my tenure at the company was ending, I started my job search. The day I was told my services were no longer needed was during a pay cycle. My manager told me I did not need to finish working until the next pay date and I was given six weeks of severance pay. On my last official day as a salaried employee, I was offered a new position. Therefore, I moved easily from one company to the next and was able to save my severance package.

Before the second layoff, in 2007, I had known there was a 50/50 chance I would be let go because another company had acquired ours. As an IT Director, I was told once again to give my work to one of my peers. Then I knew my days were short. Luckily, due to my position in the company, I was given a 6-month severance package, outplacement services, and I was able to cash my stock options. In addition, about five months prior, I had earned a bonus worth 45% of my base salary. So I had enough money in the bank to survive without a job for two years. Therefore, I honestly thought I was going to be fine.

Three years and five months went by without a full-time job. I was running through my savings at an alarming rate. I scaled back on expenses, but I was too prideful to seek assistance from the government, my church, or non-profit organizations until it was too late. I almost lost my home to foreclosure three times. I exhausted all my disposable cash, savings, retirement, stocks, bonds, and unemployment benefits. I was a lost soul with a pseudo plan and limited direction.

Finally, in January 2011, I accepted a position only to be laid off a third time in June 2012. This time I was determined not to make the same mistakes. I was offered a two-week severance package, but negotiated a third. I was wise enough by then to know the three-week severance package would not last me three weeks. That money was gone before I deposited it into my bank account. Bills were already due. I was left with zero money in the bank, zero savings, no retirement account, and no disposable cash. It felt like rock bottom. But I was determined to turn this third job layoff into a positive experience. I refused to consider borrowing money from family and friends. I needed to figure out how to get beyond the day of that third layoff.

Like most people, every time my job ended I rushed home to update my resume, cover letter, and start my job search without thinking about the change holistically. On a scale of 1 to 10 with 10 being highest, my competitive score is 10. Therefore, I devised a plan to submit my resume to 100 companies within 10 days, and I was determined to secure a job within one month of my layoff. I would get up every morning and start my job search. I took meticulous notes and waited for the phone to start ringing. I had a mental image of recruiters calling me day and night for interviews. After the first week with not a single call, I started to make excuses. "I'm sure the recruiters are busy." The second week passed without the phone ringing. I started to wonder what was going on. A third week had me asking myself what was wrong with the recruiters. I was a professional with solid training and 20 years experience. I could not believe I was not in hot demand. The fourth week I finally received one phone call for a face-to-face interview. I did not get that job, or the next three.

My spirit was crushed. I felt like an athlete who'd just come in last place. I did not know what else to do. All my plans had failed. I was left with a fight for which I was not prepared. My emotions drained me. Defeat loomed over my head. I faced rock bottom again. Then the warrior in me started to rise up. I thought, if I have to fight, then I am going out in a blaze of glory.

While I worked as an IT Director for the company that laid me off the second time in 2007, as I said, I knew there was a 50/50 chance I could be laid off. But other members of my team were also in jeopardy and some of them had not worked for another company in 15-20 years so they were not prepared to search for a new job. Therefore, within my department I developed a program titled "Getting Beyond the Day: How to Prepare for a Workplace Layoff." As a leader, I felt it was my responsibility to equip the team members with skills needed to prepare themselves just in case they were laid off. I had plans to implement workshops on resumes and how to dress for success, and even to conduct mock interviews. However, before I could fully execute the program, I received my "pink slip" and was escorted out the door.

After that month of looking for a job with no offers, I had to figure out how I was going to pay my mortgage payment, my medical, dental, and vision bills, insurance premiums, utilities, etc., etc., etc. Also, I needed to figure out what I was going to do about college for my son. He had been an "A" student all the years of his academic life and had been accepted into a top university. So there was no way I was going to turn to him and say, "Josh, I'm sorry, but you no longer can go to college because I lost my job." Therefore, I had no choice but to figure out how I was going to get beyond the day.

I decided I was going to dust off that program I had planned back in 2007 and implement it for myself. Then it occurred to me that I should document what I learned in a book for others to use during a job layoff. Therefore, out of a dark, painful place in my life when I had been near rock bottom, but was determined to go out fighting, this book was born. I was going to fight for my life, my son, and my sanity with all I had in me.

With my new vision to figure out how to move forward, I came up with the following list of areas where I needed help:

- Mortgage Assistance
- Medical Provision
- Continued Training
- College Tuition Assistance
- Business Opportunities

Then I came up with a completely separate list of things that would be needed if my profile were slightly different. My initial list fit my needs as a single mother with a child ready for college, but I started thinking about single mothers with small children who would need childcare assistance, people who were disabled, veterans, senior citizens, and more. I knew the book could not be just about me. I knew I had to think about other people and how a job layoff would affect their unique lives. At that moment, I realized I had not hit rock bottom. I remembered a Bible study teacher who used to tell me, "Your vision is greater than your circumstance." Therefore, the book took on a completely new meaning for me. I was determined to become this book in the flesh (by implementing appropriate action items) and help others who may not have my same profile, but who needed other types of assistance.

With my laptop, the Internet, and my vision of helping others as well as myself, I expanded my list of five items into over 20. I started researching what support was available for people who were unemployed, and I was blown away by the resources I found. I quickly started to apply for various programs and learned that the process was relatively easy and painless.

After about a month of working on the book by myself, I was introduced to a woman and we agreed to have lunch together a few days later. As I thought about it, I had no clue why we had decided to meet, but we had arranged it, so I went. I often have many different projects in the works, so So I printed out various projects I had going on to see what I could discuss with her. As we started sharing what each of us was doing, she mentioned she was a professional resume writer and more. At that moment, I knew why I had been destined to meet her. She was the perfect person to co-author *Getting Beyond the Day*. I asked if she would be interested in helping me write a book to assist people who were unemployed. She quickly answered, "Yes." Therefore, Jill and I joined forces on this project. Later, she told me she did not hesitate because she not only understood my reality; she also recognized that thousands of others needed guidance concerning this workplace hazard. She thought my book idea would provide peace and empowerment, a positive solution.

There is always a light at the end of the tunnel. My journey of writing this book really started when I first started working after college. Throughout the last twenty years, I have found myself expendable three times, and even as a hiring manager Jill has found herself in that place as well. With each layoff, the emotions that ran through me were the same. I even felt some of the same things when it was my peers and direct reports that were laid off. Now more than ever, I understand it is what we do after that day that determines what comes next.

News flash! The main reason a company is in business is to make money. The sooner you accept that your job layoff was not personal, the faster you will move through the emotional changes you are experiencing.

Life-changing events are marked by a day. Whether it is the loss of a loved one, a marriage, a divorce, a job layoff, or you find out about an illness, you need to be prepared for change. "Getting Beyond the Day™ is just that — a guidebook to empower dislocated workers with resources and tools needed to move past the day and get their lives back on track.

During my third layoff, I started to reflect on why it is difficult for us as loyal, hardworking employees to accept a layoff and not take it personally. I resolved that since birth we have been told the "who, what, when, where, why, and how" in life. When we were born, our pediatricians gave our parent(s) a schedule (a plan) to follow as we grew. Then in elementary school, our teachers gave us a curriculum (a plan) for us to follow to successfully move to the next grade. Then in high school our teachers gave us a curriculum (a plan) to reach graduation. After graduation, we were told to 1) get a job, 2) attend college, 3) attend a trade school, or 4) go into the military. Once on the job, in college, in trade school, or in the military, we were told the "who, what, when, where, why, and how" (a plan) to be successful as adults.

Now, all of a sudden comes the news that you have been laid off, fired, downsized, etc. Your identity is gone. Your "plan" no longer exists. There is no doctor, no teacher, no parent, no instructor, no college professor, no military officer, no boss to give you the plan (the "who, what, when, where, why, and how"). Feeling defeated with emotions running through your body that you did not know existed, you are left with emptiness. There are no words in the English dictionary to describe how you feel.

As of the writing of this book, the unemployment rate in America is 7.8%. Home foreclosure rates are in double digits. There is a vast amount of information out there to help people who are unemployed and at risk of losing their homes. The problem is how to find it. This book targets all those who have lost their jobs or been selected for layoff. Through the various tips contained herein, it also relates to individuals who just want to save money by cutting their personal/home expenses.

Job loss is one of the most significant stresses a person can face. Upon learning about a layoff, almost every area of your life is affected. While each person is impacted in unique ways, certain areas of life are inevitably changed to some degree or other.

As you process the news of a job layoff, Getting Beyond the Day™ is a roadmap to help you stay focused on finding your next career move, but also addressing all of the other aspects of your life. It contains valuable resources to pursue as aids during your time of unemployment. Use the Getting Beyond the Day™ Workbook as your daily notebook to keep track of your accomplishments and "to do" items. The book is broken down into three main sections: Career, Family, and Life, with resources relating to each and words of wisdom from a hiring manager, an HR representative, an executive, and a person who has been unemployed in his career. In addition, the appendices offer other tips.

In offering this book, Jill and I want to deliver a message of hope to you, the reader, to provide tools and resources to empower you, and to give you a strategy (a plan) to move forward.

Breakthrough is imminent,
Nicole Antoinette
Victory of the People, Beyond Praise!

Fight another Fight to Dream another Dream

HOW TO USE THIS BOOK

Getting Beyond the Day™ - Your Guide to Surviving a Job Layoff has three main sections. Each focuses on a different aspect of your essential needs as a professional. Readers are expected to review and be familiar with the contents of this book.

CAREER

In this section you find topics to assist in your career development as it pertains to an occupation or a profession.

FAMILY

In this section you find topics to assist you and your family.

LIFE

In this section you find topics to assist in general life areas.

There are three ways we recommend you use this guidebook:

USE BY PROFILE

The Use by Profile describes you at a high level based upon the following:

- Marital Status (Single, Married, Widow, Divorced)
- Gender
- Family Status (Number of Children)
- Age Group (20s, 30s, 40s, 50s, Senior Citizen)
- Social Class (Lower, Middle, Upper)
- Veteran
- Disabled
- Entrepreneur
- Housing Status (Own, Rent)

Based upon your profile, you can view the Table of Contents for topics that are relevant for your profile. Here is an example of Nicole Antoinette's profile:

- Single
- Female
- One child in college
- Early 40s
- Middle Class
- Entrepreneur
- Homeowner

Based upon the profile of Nicole Antoinette, here are the topics she would review in the book:

- Entrepreneur
- Financial Assistance
- Health Care
- Home Improvements
- Housing
- Networking
- Social Media

USE BY NEEDS

A needs analysis will provide you with concrete data to effectively use this book. If you take the time to conduct this review, you will be able to select topics for you to review. Here is an example of Nicole Antoinette's needs analysis:

- Mortgage Assistance
- Medical Provision
- Continued Training
- College Tuition Assistance
- Business Opportunities

Therefore, based upon the needs of Nicole Antoinette, here are the topics she would review in the book:

- Entrepreneur
- Financial Assistance
- Health Care
- Housing
- Networking
- Social Media

USE BY ICONS

Throughout this book, you will find icons that represent special content the authors want to bring to your attention.

The "Tips" icon represents quick points to remember on a particular topic.

The "For Your Information (FYI)" icon represents points of interest about a topic that do not require any action to be performed.

The "Important" icon represents HOT topics to which you will need to pay close attention.

The "Case Study" icon represents real-life examples.

The "Warning" icon represents information about a certain action or behavior to watch out for.

The "Words of Wisdom" icon represents knowledge based upon life experiences.

Fight another Fight to Dream another Dream

CONTENTS

WHAT TO DO ON LAYOFF DAY

When an employer decides to lay off workers, the company generally performs a thorough "due diligence" for weeks in order to maintain the security of its property, as well as to ensure that its legal rights are protected. As the employee experiencing the layoff you need to ensure you understand your rights and plan to protect yourself as well.

Here are some examples of how employers protect themselves during layoffs that can cause you to lose benefits or other opportunities to which you are entitled:

- Employers will offer the employee the option to resign – Most professional employees will accept this offer because they do not want to have record of an involuntary termination from a prior job. However, an employee "forced to resign" may be entitled to such benefits

FOR YOUR INFO

An employee who "voluntarily" resigns his/her employment is not entitled to unemployment insurance benefits.

- Arbitration Agreement – If you did not sign an Arbitration Agreement during your employment an employer may request that you sign one before termination.

- Confidentiality/Non-Solicitation Agreements – If you did not sign a Confidentiality/Non-Solicitation Agreement an employer may request that you sign one before termination.

IMPORTANT

NOTE: Consult an attorney before signing legal documents. Do not sign anything under pressure the day you are laid off.

It is important to remember that you will not think straight when you are told the news of a layoff. When an employer requests you to sign a severance agreement, disciplinary report, or other paperwork they have just placed in front of you take a deep breath and ask for a copy to review. Look at it once you have had a chance to calm down.

IMPORTANT

If there is anything you do not understand take it to a lawyer to have it reviewed before you sign. You may be giving up rights you should not, or maybe you have some advantage to negotiate for more money.

You especially do not want to sign a Non-Solicitation Agreement that limits your ability to work for a year or two unless you understand it and are getting some substantial dollars for it.

YOUR COURSE OF ACTION CHECKLIST

Here is a quick reference of things to do to help you think clearly when you get the news that you have been fired or laid off:

- ☐ Download your Employee Contact List
- ☐ Obtain a copy of the Employee Handbook
- ☐ Download the company phone list
- ☐ Retrieve personal information on the company's computer
- ☐ Obtain a copy of the Separation Notice Form
- ☐ Obtain a copy of the Layoff Letter
- ☐ Request your last paycheck and/or severance pay
- ☐ Ask for a Letter of Recommendation
- ☐ Obtain a copy of your Benefits Status Letter
- ☐ Wages
  - Determine what "wages" are owed to you (NOTE: Laws vary by state)
  - Consider past practices, verbal commitments, any written documents, or e-mail correspondence, what is stated in the offer letter/employment agreement, company policies, or any handbook, etc.
  - Determine when wages must be paid following termination (NOTE: Laws vary by state)
  - Determine if deductions are necessary for unpaid loans, wage overpayments, lost or stolen company property, and whether those deductions are allowed by law
- ☐ Vacation
  - How much vacation did you earn?
  - How much vacation did you use?
  - Is the company required to pay you for accrued, but unused vacation?
    - ❖ What is the company's policy (handbook, offer letter, past practice, etc.)?
    - ❖ What is required by the law of the state in which (a) the company operates and (b) the employee resides? (NOTE: Laws vary by state)

❏ Options/Restricted Stock/Other Securities of the Company

- Were any securities granted?
- What is outstanding? What is vested? What is forfeited?
- Does anything additional vest as a result of the termination?
- How long do you have to exercise any option to purchase?
- Does the company have any repurchase obligations? If so, will the company exercise those rights? If so, when is the deadline?
- Is a notice regarding your rights and obligations required?

❏ Continued Health Insurance Coverage Notice (COBRA)

❏ Employee Benefits

- Obtain the Retirement plan rollover information
- Determine if any action should be taken regarding any applicable medical reimbursement or dependent care reimbursement plan

❏ Expense Reports – Submit final expense report (*if applicable*)

❏ Timesheet– Submit final timesheet (*if applicable*)

❏ Termination Meeting/Exit Interview

- Discuss appropriate details regarding termination (effective date, business reasons for termination, pay and benefits after termination, if any, unemployment eligibility, etc.)
- Review confidentiality or proprietary information agreement
- Discuss inventions (*if applicable*)
- Confirm your address for future mailing of information
- Obtain information for a contact person and information for questions arising after the meeting

NOTE: Some of these items on the checklist require you to return to your computer. If you are escorted out of the building immediately you can ask a co-worker to assist or ask your hiring manager.

4 • • • • • • • • • • • • • • • •

BEYOND THE LAYOFF

Are you wondering why this happened to you since you outperformed everyone on your team, but some of them are still working? Is it the first time you have left your home, and even then, a well-meaning friend coaxed you? Perhaps the whole experience is all still surreal and your mind is telling you your severance will not last forever. Yes, your heart is indeed still beating, but oh, the pain still cuts and swirls like a blade of a circular saw. Let us look at today...anew.

You have lost something precious to you, and you are experiencing the loss of it.

Grief. All these emotions are cycles and phases you will likely experience and endure because you definitely lost a major part of your life: your livelihood.

In this section you will learn:

- The five stages of change
- The signs or symptoms of each phase
- What to do about them

UNEMPLOYED

Experts say each person may not experience each stage in the order presented. The length of unemployment may determine how long the cycle lasts or whether you undergo it more than once.

Acceptance Stage: Perhaps you are in this phase now since you are reading this book. It shows you not only recognize your job status, but you are on a mission to change it. Perhaps your mantra should now be, "My unemployment status will not last forever." You will be hired again — if you apply for positions. Yes, it takes time, but you will succeed. Is there a bad side to it? Unfortunately, in this economic climate, there is. You may be someone, or perhaps you know someone, who has lost a job more than once. The key is to believe the job status will change. You can and will bounce back.

Bargaining Stage: When your former supervisor and/or Human Resources department informed you of your layoff, did you volunteer to take a cut in pay or work in another part of the company? This is a sign of bargaining to salvage or change a decision that has already been made for you. Sure, it makes you feel helpless and not in control of your own life. You probably feel you left your identity in their office. You did not, unless you give them that power. If you did, reinvent yourself and be that much better for it.

Denial Stage: Have you told anyone the truth about your job status? Do you keep telling yourself you will wait until tomorrow to launch your job quest, yet somehow your severance and unemployment benefits have dwindled to where you only have two weeks left to draw? You are most likely in the denial stage. This has never happened to you before, so it is understandable. Know two things: 1) You will find another job, and 2) You will not find another job unless you search for it. It is okay not to have the same job you once had. Do not think of yourself as a title. Think of yourself as someone who is willing to overcome, survive, and reinvent. Take pride in that person you become.

Depression Stage: This phase often includes physical symptoms such as fatigue, irritability, loss of interest in things you once enjoyed, and headaches. It often lasts longer depending on how long you go without a job. How do you move forward when you do not even want to talk to anybody or get out of bed?

If your symptoms are severe please seek professional counseling immediately. This book lists a number of free-to-low-cost options at the end of this chapter under *Counseling Options.*

Anger Stage: If you are the kind of employee who always gives 110% you may feel this emotion first, even if you knew layoffs were coming. In all honesty, there may be two reasons you were laid off: 1) Your position truly needed to be eliminated for business and financial reasons, or 2) You no longer fit your division's specific job culture. In the past, all you had to do was to perform well. Part of overcoming this emotion is recognizing that there needed to be layoffs and there is always a list of names...plural. Do not suppress your anger. Work through it in positive ways. Experts suggest natural methods of relieving aggression such as a friendly game of tennis or boxing lessons from a friend (so they are free), or journaling.

LAYOFF SURVIVORS

Sometimes the people you show the most anger toward are those who remain in the workplace: the survivors of the layoffs.

Experts say they, too, go through the same cycles of change. Why? They, too, witnessed everyone receiving the "call of doom," and waited and wondered if they would be next. When they were told they would be staying they wondered not only if they would be good enough to fill the void left by those who were released, but also if they were best suited to doing the jobs of so many. Often they do not want their new job responsibilities and feel guilty because they know you and others are struggling now.

They may experience the stages in these ways:

Anger: Management may treat them as if they should be grateful for their jobs, not realizing they are not only performing new positions or doing the work of many, but are also grieving the loss of you and others. Companies have to keep the business running, and they often do not train the survivors for their new responsibilities. Companies give you bereavement time for a relative, but never for a friend who was laid off. Psychologists say the grieving process is the same.

Bargaining: They may have asked to be transferred to another position or division, just as you did, depending on their levels of authority or agenda.

Denial: They may not understand what their status is now. Yes, they still have a job, but they may not understand how unstable the company or their position really is. This could paralyze their work performance. The very thing that kept their positions secure during previous layoffs could put them in line to be eliminated if there is further downsizing.

Acceptance: The layoff survivor who accepts the situation is someone who not only takes newfound responsibilities in stride, but also makes plans for the future.

Depression: Yes, people who survive layoffs may go through bouts of depression, too. Consider how his or her whole world has changed as well, and everyone, including you, handles change differently. They, too, may need counseling.

COUNSELING OPTIONS

There are a number of free resources and counseling options if you need to discuss any of these emotions with a professional. Do not be ashamed to seek help. Your situation is only temporary. The sooner you seek assistance the more quickly you will be on your path to success.

Freementalhealth.com. If you scroll down and click the anxiety and depression link you can type in your zip code to find resources that either treat people with depression or can recommend places that can handle it; all free. If your depression has led to substance abuse there are clinics that treat that as well. The site also has links for referrals that may charge a small fee.

Nami.org. The National Alliance on Mental Illness posts information on its website about depression and other emotions described in this book. It also gives access to numbers in your area to get counseling.

Training and research hospitals: If you live in or near a town with a training or research hospital, know that it may provide opportunities for you to seek treatment as one of its training clinic participants.

United Way: This organization provides family and individual counseling. An easy way to remember is to dial 2-1-1 or visit the website at 211.org.

The YWCA/YMCA: This organization may charge a fee, but it will not turn anyone away for non-payment. In short, you can arrange a payment plan if you prefer its services.

8 ● ● ● ● ● ● ● ● ● ● ● ● ● ● ●

TOP FIVE MYTHS

If you are newly unemployed you may have some preconceived notions about the days ahead. This section is designed to dispel the biggest myths.

1. **Myth:** You are always eligible for unemployment insurance.

   Reality: There are a number of reasons you may not qualify for unemployment. If you are unsure check benefits.gov. This resource may reveal many benefits you may not have considered.

2. **Myth:** You should spend all your time job-searching.

   Reality: You can present your best when there is balance in your life. Yes, absolutely schedule time for job-searching, but also make time for friends, family, relaxation, and fun. This book's Daily Routine section offers suggestions on the best way to plan your day.

3. **Myth:** Apply for any and everything you see that is available.

   Reality: Focus your search, just as you would if you were conducting your job quest at any other time in your career This book's Job Search and Bridge Job sections lists resources to help you with your mission to find your highly coveted job.

4. **Myth:** Nobody can tell you are going through the stages of change (anger, depression, etc.).

   Reality: Your closest family and friends will be able to tell. Make sure you do not lash out at the ones who support you the most. What you are feeling is indeed real and should not be suppressed, but there are positive ways to do it. The Stages of Change are discussed in detail in this book as well as counseling options.

5. **Myth:** You can snap out of it and find a job quickly.

   Reality: You should not suppress your emotions. As of this writing, on average, 3,000 people per day lose their jobs. So many people in the market for jobs makes competition fierce. It does not mean you will never find a job. Finding one quickly, however, without taking drastic steps and networking, is nearly impossible. Never say never. There are exceptions to every rule. That is why there are innovators and pioneers. Reinvention and Networking are both discussed in detail in this book, which is intended to be a message of hope.

DOCUMENTATION CHECKLIST

According to Lorie Marrero, CPO, professional organizer and creator of ClutterDiet.com, "Disorganization creates stress because it reflects that there are commitments in your life that you simply can't handle."

While you are looking for a job or working on your next career move, it is important to gather personal documents and make copies to have on hand when needed:

- ☐ 60-90 days of pay check stubs
- ☐ A statement of how living expenses are being paid
- ☐ Address verification (utility bills, voter registration card, state issued ID)
- ☐ Alien registration number and expiration date, if a non-citizen
- ☐ Bank statements (personal and business)
- ☐ Benefits Status Letter
- ☐ Bills
  - Account number
  - Login ID
  - Password
  - Website
  - Phone number
- ☐ Birth certificate
- ☐ Cover letter
- ☐ DD Form 214 if you have served in the military in the last 18 months
- ☐ Department of Labor Claims Examiner's Determination
- ☐ Disconnect notices for utilities (electronic, gas, water)
- ☐ Driver's license or ID card number
- ☐ Employment history
- ☐ Federal Tax Returns for last two years
- ☐ Federal Tax Transcripts for last two years
- ☐ Hardship letter

DOCUMENTATION CHECKLIST

10

- ☐ Insurance cards (medical, dental, vision, car)
- ☐ Layoff letter
- ☐ Letter(s) of Recommendation
- ☐ Living expenses
- ☐ Mortgage statement for last three months
- ☐ Personal references
- ☐ Previous year's W-2 form(s)
- ☐ Professional references
- ☐ Profit & Loss Statement for last year and year to date (if applicable)
- ☐ Proof of death or divorce (if applicable)
  - Death certificate
  - Divorce papers
- ☐ Proof to Work in the United States (based upon your personal status)
  - Birth certificate
  - U.S. Passport
  - Resident Alien card
  - Unexpired Employment Authorization Document that contains a photograph
  - School record (if place of birth is shown)
  - DD214 (if place of birth is shown)
- ☐ Property Tax Statement
- ☐ Reduction in hours letter from employer
- ☐ Release Agreement
- ☐ Rental history
- ☐ Resume
- ☐ Salary history
- ☐ Separation notice from employer
- ☐ Social Security Card
- ☐ Unemployment Insurance Benefit determination

RESOURCE CHECKLIST

Until you decide on your next career move, looking for a new position can seem like a full-time job. Since most companies provide the necessities to perform a job function (e.g., pens, paper, copy machine, printer, etc.), while you are temporarily on your own, it is important to create an office space in your home or apartment equipped with supplies.

- ❏ Binders
- ❏ Calculator
- ❏ Calendar
- ❏ Chair
- ❏ Computer
- ❏ Desk
- ❏ Email account
- ❏ Envelopes
- ❏ File cabinet
- ❏ File folders
- ❏ Flash drive
- ❏ Garbage can
- ❏ Highlighters
- ❏ Hole punch
- ❏ Internet
- ❏ Lamp
- ❏ Manila folders
- ❏ Memo board
- ❏ Notepads
- ❏ Paper

- ❏ Paper clips
- ❏ Paper shredder
- ❏ Pencils
- ❏ Pens
- ❏ Phone
- ❏ Print cartridges
- ❏ Printer/Copier/ Scanner/Fax Machine
- ❏ Return address labels
- ❏ Ruler
- ❏ Scissors
- ❏ Shelving
- ❏ Sign Here stickers
- ❏ Stamps
- ❏ Staple remover
- ❏ Stapler
- ❏ Staples
- ❏ Sticky notepads
- ❏ Tape

12 • • • • • • • • • • • • • •

DAILY ROUTINE

How do you spend your day?

> **IMPORTANT**
>
> The best thing you can do for yourself to move forward is establish a daily routine.

Eat nutritious meals and exercise to stay alert and healthy. This will not only enhance your mood, but will reduce the need for doctors and consequently bills.

Get dressed, even if all you do all day is read emails. This becomes part of your daily routine. Showering and dressing as if you are meeting friends will make you feel better. Try to rise and go to bed at the same time every day. This will help you to structure your day.

Set a schedule of when you will look for jobs. You can vary your routine from day to day. For example, perhaps Mondays you will only conduct online searches. Tuesdays you will make cold calls and network. Wednesdays you will look for new leads through your social media channels, etc. Soon you will want to do all these in one day as you start to get responses.

Make sure your schedule includes time with others. You do not want to become a hermit or start to withdraw. This could be simply making time for your family or making sure you network once a week.

Do something that is both creative and beneficial to you. For example, if you find time to volunteer it can help you and others. That volunteer activity can always lead to a part-time or full-time position. Even if it does not it is certainly something you should immediately include on your resume. Potential employers want to know you have been doing something with your time, not how long you have been unemployed.

If you do all these things every day you will find your time passes quickly. Rather than sitting around waiting on anybody, you regain control of that aspect of your life.

THE BRIDGE JOB

TIP

An approach to carry you through a difficult employment or financial period is to implement a "Bridge Job" strategy.

Does that mean it is okay to say "no" to a job offer when you are unemployed? You always have that option. Understand, however, that showing on your resume that you have worked may make a difference. And having that cash flow adds up to help you over rough waters until the "right" job comes along. So you may have to take it. The way to show up with a great attitude is to pursue the right job in the first place.

You never know when that in-between job — that "bridge" job — may really be the one that lands you a position beyond your dreams. Typically, the term means the job before retirement, but if you are just laid off or in transition view it as a temporary assignment before the one you really want.

You may have read or heard about the federal government's "Bridge to Work" programs. As of this writing, zero states have applied for its plan, which is reportedly modeled after Georgia's program listed below. Critics say there were not enough proven results, although a third of the initial workforce reportedly was hired. Below are details about Georgia's program and one in Connecticut.

Georgia Works: This program calls for an unemployed person to train on a job for eight weeks, 24 hours or less per week. In exchange, the participant does not get a salary, but will receive unemployment benefits plus a $240 stipend. There is no guarantee of being hired, but the training can be included on his/her resume. Here is the link for more details: dol.state.ga.us/em/georgia_works.

Platform to Employment: This Connecticut program takes an applicant through a five-week assessment and coaching experience. After satisfactory completion the participant is allowed to train on the job for eight weeks. The Workplace, a partner of America's Workforce Network, subsidizes the trainee's wages. More details can be found by visiting its website at: platformforemployment.com.

In writing this book, our research revealed the story of a person who suffered an unexpected layoff. No warning, no plan. With a great attitude, he maintained communication with his former boss and trustworthy friends as he searched for a job every day. It paid off in the form of smaller temporary assignments that eventually put him in a position that was better than the one he lost.

The "Drawbridge": His first paying job was contract work. He was hired to work on a steady basis, but only for a specific amount of time. While this position utilized some of his skill set, it certainly did not pay him at normal rate. This created difficulties. Such a position feels like a drawbridge. You are taking what you perceive as less money. But remember, a job means some money. In this case, he learned new skills, which set him up for the next temporary assignment. Acquiring new skills on the job is always a bonus.

The "Suspension" Bridge: Next, he landed a full-time job with benefits. It felt to him like a wide beam over water. Why? He went to work feeling no job was perfect every day. He applied himself by initiating projects that were not part of his job description. That demonstrated his creativity. Still, no manager seemed to notice or care. That did not stop him, though, because this, by definition, was his passion. He had to do it.

The Span: The distance between one end of a bridge and the other is called a span. He reached the end of his span when an external force noticed his passion. He had never even imagined the job his creativity opened for him, and yet, it was the end of his bridge and the start of his journey to his new dream career. He said he never would have reached that point if all the other factors and jobs had not occurred first.

The Teachable Moment: During the job quest, he asked for help and nearly all those he reached out to gave it when they could. Not everyone? No. Some people think being unemployed could never happen to them and so do not bother helping others. But as you know, unemployment does not discriminate according to color, gender, or title. In this case, one of the same people who refused to help ended up losing his job, too. Interestingly, he in turn asked the main subject of our story for help. Oh, the audacity! He had not provided a helping hand when needed. What would you have done? Our subject chose to help, but simply mentioned what had happened when the roles had been reversed. He did not dwell on the issue or prolong it, but he did not let it go without mention, either. He chose to help because negativity is contagious, but positive action truly makes a difference in all our lives.

WORDS OF WISDOM One of the most devastating events in a person's life is losing a job. After dealing with the various results of change which include shock, numbness, denial, fear, or anger, the next phase is simply to "move-on." Moving on sounds very simple, yet it is profound. As an HR professional, I would offer three suggestions to a displaced worker.

1. Have your resume professionally prepared by a reputable and experienced company. Many times people let friends or family members create or update their resumes because they are articulate or write pretty good, however they still lack the knowledge and experience of choosing the correct language or key words that should appear on a resume.

2. Network! Networking is the oldest method of finding a job In the mid 90s the internet became the next great phenomenon with employers having the ability to post vacant positions on their corporate websites. This gave potential candidates the opportunity to post their resumes. Over time, it has proven true that networking – reaching out and staying connected to old friends, family members, former co-workers, and civic or professional organizations – always yields highest results in landing that next opportunity.

3. Strengthen your mind. The mind is a terrible thing to waste, so keep it sharp by reading professional and social articles, journals, books etc., volunteering, and staying active, which includes exercise. The mind can only be as strong as how well you feed it. So feed your mind with positive thoughts, visions of your next job, and the belief that you will soon return to the workforce.

HR professionals may have many recommendations, but the very best advice I would give to anyone seeking a new position is to talk to those who have been through layoffs before. Listen and learn from their experience. And above all, have much faith. Without it we cannot do anything!

Arthur R. Reese III, PHR, HR Business Consultant
PhD candidate, Industrial and Organizational Psychology, Capella University
M.S. Human Resources Management and Development, National Louis University
BBA Business Administration, Georgia Southern University

Fight another Fight to Dream another Dream

SECTION ONE

CAREER

Fight another Fight to Dream another Dream

1-1 CAREER OPTIONS

Are you feeling that your career is now over? Worse, do you think you have no options? In this section, you will:

- Consider alternatives to your career track
- Assess whether a career change is right for you
- Gain knowledge about free online career assessment tools

HOW TO REINVENT YOURSELF

The first strategy to success at this point in your life is to invest in yourself. You must believe you will succeed. You have to reach a point at which the alternative is not an option. That does not mean you are not stressed. It simply means you are driven, and nothing else matters. You have the desire to succeed. After you embrace this point of view, all advice may seem easy because you will want to do whatever it takes.

Here are seven options for you to try. Not all are feasible for everyone because some people want to remain employees while others refuse to work for anyone else ever again. Not sure what to do? Do not worry. We have help for you, too.

Contact Former Bosses: One of the best things you can do for yourself is to tell people — specifically former bosses or hiring managers with whom you still have a good rapport — that you are now looking for a job. Do not feel you are wearing a badge of shame. What better person to speak accolades about you? Consider this a word-of-mouth (or online) strategy that could land you a job...again.

Train Others: Just because you can no longer perform your duties at your former company does not mean there is no longer a need for that skill. Consider training others to work in your industry as an instructor at a continuing education center, a teacher at a high school, or even in the form of a consultant. Some of these may require gaining a certification, but some businesses and organizations will take the time to certify you.

Take It Down a Notch: Pursue jobs you may be overqualified for but might enjoy to at least earn a paycheck. Do not limit yourself to positions in your field. Consider those you have always wanted to do such as work in a shoe or fashion retail store for the employee discounts.

Consider Temporary Work: Temporary agency assignments and seasonal work are always options if you just need money to get you beyond the day, week, and month. Everyone has a transferrable skill set. It is time to stop thinking of yourself as just a person with a former title. Instead, focus on skills such as communication, conflict resolution, or even administration that may have landed you your first job, but that you also perfected over the years.

Plot Your Day: This option may not be for everyone, especially with certain physical conditions, but for some, day or manual labor can be added to the list of options. If the work is there, do not discount this idea.

Work for Yourself: Many financial experts say the economy is perfect for starting your own business. If you have acquired enough skills to charge others for your services, do it! If you tell business associations your circumstances some may even give you a break on the fee to join. In certain states, Google offers a free website for business owners. Check out gybo. com/georgia. In numerous states and cities, veterans who are business owners also get free benefits.

Retrain, Get a Grant: The Workforce Investment Act is now in effect, which gives states more than $2.9 billion to allow laid-off workers to retrain in the computer technology, healthcare, and renewable energy industries. In short, you could get a small grant to go back to school to retrain in these fields.

CAREER CONFUSION

Are you still unclear about what path to ultimately take? Did your passion die the day you walked out of your company? You have to be careful to make sure it is not the people holding you back instead of what you once did for a living. Ask yourself: What motivates you to get up in the morning, in terms of a profession? Is there a job out there that you would fight to have? Is there one you feel so strongly about that you would vote to remove an elected official if he or she made it illegal to do? That is passion.

AVAILABLE RESOURCES

To help you understand yours, perhaps a career assessment is something you need to do. Some free online tools are CoachCompass.com and the University of Waterloo Career Services.

You can also get free career guidance at government agencies.

Career One Stop: Just like its name, you can do everything career-related by visiting this website, http://www.careeronestop.org/.

Employment & Training Administration: If you are looking for information about grants, this U.S. Department of Labor's site, http://www.doleta.gov/, is the place to go.

My Skills My Future: My Skills My Future's site, http://www.myskillsmyfuture.org/, allows you to put your last job title and skills into its system to find the best careers for you. It is that simple.

Occupational Outlook Handbook: Occupational Outlook Handbook is another agency site, http://www.bls.gov/ooh/, that offers details about jobs nationwide, and the training and education needed to obtain them.

1-2 COVER LETTER

Has it been a long while since you have had to even think about a cover letter because you have not had to submit a resume anywhere? In this age of computerized gatekeepers and key words, some even debate whether anyone reads cover letters anymore. However, many hiring managers say they use all avenues to weed out applicants now that hundreds are vying for the same positions. In short, your cover letter may make the difference between obtaining a job interview and having your resume ignored. You should devote the necessary time and effort to writing an effective cover letter.

How much do you say in a cover letter? The answer is simple. In this section, you will learn:

- A 3-paragraph formula that will make employers want to read your resume
- How much you should reveal about your circumstances
- The essential elements of the generic cover letter template

TELL YOUR NEWS

Realize that downsizing and layoffs happen to the best workers. Employers do not frown at that. Failure to do anything afterward is the problem. With that said, know that, yes, you can and should mention that your job was eliminated, but proudly emphasize in your cover letter what you have been doing since that day. Make it concise and relate what you can do for your potential employer. This can be what gets you hired, in the end, but it should not be your lead.

The lead paragraph should detail why you are writing and why you chose this company to pursue.

Finally, tell the potential hiring manager how to reach you. If you write with passion and show the benefits of hiring you, chances are the employer will definitely read your resume. Remember, that is part of the point: to entice the hiring manager to read the resume. Consequently, you do not want your cover letter to be entirely repetitive of your resume. Both, of course, should be well written.

SAMPLE COVER LETTER

Your Name
Email address
Phone number

Date

Mr./Ms. Hiring Manager, Title
Company
Address
City, State Zip

Dear Mr./Ms. _____:

I am writing to express my interest in your _____ position. I believe _____, _____ and _____ are essential traits to succeed in this industry. I know your company has the same philosophy, and that is one of the many reasons I want to be part of your team.

I have enclosed my resume for your review. You will find that I have:
• _____ years of experience.
• Increased revenue by _____.
• Decreased costs by _____.

I can also add _____ because I have been spending my time _____ after a workplace layoff.

If my background fits your criteria, please do not hesitate to call or email me at the contact information listed above. I will contact you on _____ to make sure you received my materials. Thanks for your consideration. It is my hope that we can build a professional rapport.

Sincerely,

Name

Enclosure: Resume

1-3 DRESS THE PART

When you go for that interview you want to look the part you are hoping to fill. Unfortunately, many underemployed or unemployed people gain weight because of an increase in sedentary lifestyle and a decrease in self-esteem. One way to resolve this is to see if a local gym will give you a membership at a reduced fee. You will never know if you do not ask. Some gyms offer free or trial memberships. Only pursue ones that do not require a credit card or personal information. If they do, it means you will be charged when the trial period expires. Read the fine print for other stipulations to your satisfaction. You can hop from one to another until the free period expires or you get a job, whichever comes first. Gyms can be a good place to network, too.

If gym membership is just too costly to maintain, you can always use what you have at hand. Lunges and squats can be executed in your home while walking and jogging can be performed in your neighborhood. If you need weight training try filled water bottles for smaller weights or purchase cheap weights for more resistance. A jump rope does not cost much, either. If you have small children their hula-hoops are great exercise tools. You can do crunches just about anywhere within your home, too.

The bottom line is that a great image does not have to cost much.

 Women, "Dress for Success" is a nationwide program that offers free suits for that initial interview: that is after you have been referred by an agency and undergo an interview with the "Dress for Success" folks. After you land your job you are eligible for a second suit or career separates.

Men, you too can have a suit to wear, thanks to Men's Wearhouse. It holds an annual clothing drive and collaborates with non-profit organizations. Contact your local store for more details about each year's efforts.

1-4 EDUCATION AND TRAINING

Unemployment offers a great opportunity to retool and adjust your skill set. Taking some time to focus on refining your existing skills and learning new ones can be beneficial during your job search. A continuum of learning tells companies you care about them as prospective employers because you want to be a knowledgeable employee. And it shows you care about yourself. Here are some resources to help you continue to develop your skills:

- Workforce Investment Act (WIA) Dislocated Worker Program
- Free Application for Federal Student Aid (FAFSA)
- One-Stop Career Center System
- Occupational Safety and Health Administration (OSHA)
- Mine Safety Health Administration (MSHA)
- Trade Adjustment Assistance
- Rapid Response Services For Laid Off Workers
- Goodwill For You

WORKFORCE INVESTMENT ACT (WIA) DISLOCATED WORKER PROGRAM

The WIA Dislocated Workers Program assists workers who have been laid off or have been notified that they will be terminated or laid off. The Adult and Dislocated Worker Program, under Title I of the Workforce Investment Act of 1998, is designed to provide quality employment and training services to assist eligible individuals in finding and qualifying for meaningful employment, and to help employers find the skilled workers they need to compete and succeed in business.

FREE APPLICATION FOR FEDERAL STUDENT AID (FAFSA)

The office of Federal Student Aid provides grants, loans, and work-study funds for college or career school. Completing the Free Application for Federal Student Aid (FAFSA) is the first step toward getting federal aid for college, career school, or graduate school.

ONE-STOP CAREER CENTER SYSTEM

You may qualify for training programs funded by the U.S. Department of Labor. If you have been laid off from a job, contact your local One-Stop Career Centers to see if you qualify for WIA training. The Department of Labor's ETA funds job training programs to improve the employment prospects of adults, youth, and dislocated workers. Programs are aimed at boosting workers' employability and earnings and are delivered primarily by states through the One-Stop Career Center System and tailored to local economies. CareerOneStop products include:

- America's Service Locator connects individuals to employment and training opportunities available at local One-Stop Career Centers. The website provides contact information for a range of local work-related services, including unemployment benefits, career development, and educational opportunities. (ServiceLocator.org)

- America's Career InfoNet helps individuals explore career opportunities to make informed employment and education choices. The website features user-friendly occupation and industry information, salary data, career videos, education resources, self-assessment tools, career exploration assistance, and other resources that support talent development in today's fast-paced global marketplace. (CareerInfoNet.org)

- MySkills myFuture helps laid-off workers and other career changers find new occupations to explore. Users can identify occupations that require skills and knowledge similar to their current or previous jobs, learn more about these suggested matches, locate local training programs, and/or apply for jobs. (mySkillsmyFuture.org)

- Competency Model Clearinghouse provides the business community with a means to communicate its skill needs to educators and the workforce system in a common industry-driven framework. The models and other competency-based resources support development of curriculum and increased awareness of careers in high-growth industries. (CareerOneStop.org/CompetencyModel)

- Worker ReEmployment provides employment, training, and financial assistance for laid-off workers. The website includes a Job Search tool with job listings for all 50 states updated daily. Users will also find resources for getting immediate help with unemployment insurance, healthcare, and other financial needs; job searching and resume tips; changing careers and understanding transferable skills; and upgrading skills through education and training. (CareerOneStop.org/ReEmployment)

- Veterans ReEmployment is a one-stop website for employment, training, and financial help after military service. The website includes the Military-to-Civilian Job Search tool where veterans and service members can search for jobs based on the skills and experiences they gained in the military. The site also includes tips for job searching and links to national, state, and local resources specifically for veteran job seekers. (CareerOneStop. org/ReEmployment/Veterans)

OCCUPATIONAL SAFETY AND HEALTH ADMINISTRATION (OSHA)

OSHA provides training programs aimed at improving safety and health in the general workplace setting. OSHA offers a wide selection of training courses and educational programs to help broaden worker and employer knowledge on the recognition, avoidance, and prevention of safety and health hazards in their workplaces.

MINE SAFETY HEALTH ADMINISTRATION (MSHA)

MSHA provides training programs aimed at improving safety and health In the mining industry. The purpose of the Mine Safety and Health Administration is to prevent death, disease, and injury from mining and to promote safe and healthful workplaces for the Nation's miners.

TRADE ADJUSTMENT ASSISTANCE

The Trade Adjustment Assistance (TAA) Program is a federal entitlement program that assists U.S. workers who have lost or may lose their jobs because of foreign trade. This program seeks to provide adversely affected workers with opportunities to obtain the skills, credentials, resources, and support necessary to become reemployed.

The first step to receiving TAA benefits and services is to file a petition on-line or by mail with the U.S. Department of Labor (DOL). Petitions are available on-line and may be obtained at American Job Centers. The petition may be filed by:

- Three or more workers in the same firm or subdivision

- The workers' employer

- A union official or other duly authorized representative of such workers; or American Job Center operators or partners (including state workforce agencies and dislocated worker units).

Upon receiving a petition, DOL initiates an investigation to determine whether the circumstances of the layoff meet the group eligibility criteria established by the Trade Act of 1974, as amended.

RAPID RESPONSE SERVICES FOR LAID OFF WORKERS

Being laid off from your job is one of the most traumatic events you can experience in life. However, you do not need to go through this transition alone. Working with your employer, there are services and resources that can be brought to you, on site, at your company prior to your layoff date. These services and resources are part of a program called Rapid Response, which will customize services and resources to your needs and the needs of your company, with a goal of getting you back to work as soon as possible and minimizing the disruptions on your life that a layoff will cause. The Rapid Response team will provide you the means to maintain an income (unemployment insurance), information on health insurance options, access to skills upgrading and training resources, and much more. This service is extremely valuable: the earlier services are begun, the better. Services and resources vary, so be sure to attend Rapid Response sessions when they are offered so that you are aware of the full array of benefits for which you may be eligible.

GOODWILL FOR YOU

Goodwill services are customized to help you succeed. At 165 Goodwills in the United States and Canada, you can find a variety of opportunities to become job ready and advance your career.

Goodwill is committed to helping you earn a living and improve your life. A career can enable you to achieve your dreams. Goodwill services are designed to:

> **Immigrants** –help you become part of the community through language and cultural awareness classes.

> **People with criminal backgrounds** - help you reintegrate into society and become a contributing member in your local community.

> **People with disabilities** - help you live independently, get a job, and advance your career by providing access to support services, specialized

training and assistive technology.

Seniors - coordinate job readiness programs and supportive services to help you live independently, pursue your employment goals and gain economic security.

Veterans and Military Families - help you and your military spouse find employment, health services and skills for entering or reentering the workplace.

Youth - prepare you for a successful educational and financial future.

A job is only part of the solution, so Goodwill services will help you meet your basic needs and the needs of your family members — such as transportation, childcare and a safe place to live — things that are critical to everyone's success. While Goodwill does not provide all these necessities, they are committed to helping you get the resources you need for success.

WARNING

ONLINE DIPLOMA MILLS: WORTHY OR WORTHLESS?

BBB Warns Your Online Diploma Could Be a Worthless Piece of Paper

It is time to head back to school for many students, and the Better Business Bureau is warning consumers against online programs that offer fast and easy high school diplomas or college degrees. As millions struggle to find jobs, earning a diploma or an advanced degree is one way to stand out from the crowd, but some students found out the hard way that the diploma they thought they earned online was not worth the paper it was printed on.

Diploma Mills: Degrees of Deception

Are you ever tempted by an e-mail or an ad claiming you can "earn a college degree based ... on life experience"? Do not be. Chances are good the ad is from a "diploma mill," a company that offers "degrees" or certificates for a flat fee, requires little if any course work, and awards degrees based solely on life experience. Most employers and educational institutions consider it lying if you claim academic credentials you did not earn through actual course work. Federal officials say it is risky behavior: If you use a so-called "degree" from a diploma mill to apply for a job or promotion you risk not being hired, being fired, and in some cases, even prosecution.

1-5 ENTREPRENEUR

An entrepreneur is a person who organizes and manages a business undertaking. An entrepreneur sees an opportunity, makes a plan, starts the business, manages the business, and receives the profits. Entrepreneurship plays a vital role in the growth of the U.S. economy.

As you reflect during your time of layoff, one option is to become an entrepreneur. If you choose this route, here are some valuable resources to get you started:

- Small Business Administration (SBA)
- Small Business Development Center (SBDC)
- Women Business Center (WBC)
- SCORE
- Veterans Business Outreach Centers
- U.S. Export Assistance Centers
- Procurement Technical Assistance Centers
- Local Business Association

SMALL BUSINESS ADMINISTRATION (SBA)

Since its founding on July 30, 1953, the U.S. Small Business Administration has delivered millions of loans, loan guarantees, contracts, counseling sessions, and other forms of assistance to small businesses. SBA provides assistance primarily through its four programmatic functions:

Access to Capital (Business Financing)
SBA provides small businesses with an array of financing options for small businesses from the smallest needs in micro lending to substantial debt and equity investment capital (venture capital).

Entrepreneurial Development (Education, Information, Technical Assistance and Training)
SBA provides free individual face-to-face and Internet counseling for small businesses and low-cost training to nascent entrepreneurs and established small businesses in over 1,800 locations throughout the United States and U.S. territories.

Government Contracting (Federal Procurement)

In keeping with the mandate of Section 15(g) of the Small Business Act, SBA's Office of Government Contracting sets goals with other federal departments and agencies to reach the statutory goal of 23 percent in prime contract dollars to small businesses. This office also provides small businesses with subcontracting procurement opportunities, outreach programs, and training.

Advocacy (Voice for Small Business)

Created in 1978, this Office reviews Congressional legislation and testifies on behalf of small business. It also assesses the impact of the regulatory burden on behalf of small businesses. Additionally, it conducts a vast array of research on American small businesses and the small business environment. The U.S. President appoints the Chief Counsel of this office.

SMALL BUSINESS DEVELOPMENT CENTER (SBDC)

Starting a business can be a challenge, but there is help for you in your area. Small Business Development Centers (SBDCs) are partnerships primarily between the government and colleges/universities administered by the Small Business Administration and aim at giving educational services for small business owners and aspiring entrepreneurs.

Assistance from an SBDC is available to anyone interested in beginning a small business for the first time or improving or expanding an existing small business who cannot afford the services of a private consultant.

WOMEN BUSINESS CENTER (WBC)

Women's Business Centers (WBCs) represent a national network of nearly 100 educational centers designed to assist women to start and grow small businesses. WBCs operate with the mission to "level the playing field" for women entrepreneurs who still face unique obstacles in the world of business.

Through the management and technical assistance provided by the WBCs, entrepreneurs (especially women who are economically or socially disadvantaged) are offered comprehensive training and counseling on a variety of topics in many languages to help them start and grow their own businesses.

SCORE

The SCORE Association "Counselors to America's Small Business" is a nonprofit association comprised of 11,500 volunteer business counselors throughout the U.S. and its territories. SCORE members are trained to serve as counselors, advisors, and mentors to aspiring entrepreneurs and business owners. These services are offered at no fee, as a community service.

VETERANS BUSINESS OUTREACH CENTERS

The Veterans Business Outreach Program (VBOP) is designed to provide entrepreneurial development services such as business training, counseling, mentoring, and referrals for eligible veterans owning or considering a small business. The SBA has 16 organizations participating in this cooperative agreement and serving as Veterans Business Outreach Centers (VBOC).

U.S. EXPORT ASSISTANCE CENTERS

Is your small business ready to go global? It may be an easier step than you think. Advances in technology can make worldwide commerce achievable for many small businesses, depending on the goods or services you offer. If you are ready to explore the possibilities and challenges of exporting, U.S. Export Assistance Centers provide the help you need. These centers are located in major metropolitan areas throughout the United States.

Each U.S. Export Assistance Center is staffed by professionals from the SBA, the U.S. Department of Commerce, the U.S. Export-Import Bank, and other public and private organizations. Together, their mission is to provide the help you need to compete in today's global marketplace. Your local U.S. Export Assistance Center is your one-stop shop, designed to provide export assistance for your small- or medium-sized business.

PROCUREMENT TECHNICAL ASSISTANCE CENTERS

Doing business with the government is a big step to growing a business. The SBA has the resources you need.

Procurement Technical Assistance Centers (PTACs) provide local, in-person counseling and training services for you, the small business owner. They are designed to provide technical assistance to businesses that want to sell products and services to federal, state, and/or local governments. PTAC services are available either free of charge, or at a nominal cost.

LOCAL BUSINESS ASSOCIATION

Another option for those who want to work for themselves is to join a local business association. The fee is often low. These local groups offer networking opportunities, one-on-one coaching services, business training, workshops, and expo opportunities at no cost or significantly reduced rates. Once you join, get involved in one of the committees, such as hospitality or membership, for more exposure and even better experience.

This alone could boost your business and garner referral partners.

1-6 INTERVIEWING

Congratulations! You made it to the interview stage. Are your nerves calm as you prepare for the questions that are certain to arise? In this section, you will:

- Learn how to respond to various scenarios of the "layoff question"
- Learn how to prepare for the interview itself
- Know what to do after the interview is over

PRE-INTERVIEW TECHNIQUES

It is no secret that most hiring managers are looking for the person who offers the best answers during an interview without seeming rehearsed. How do you strike the right balance? You prepare, but present your knowledge authentically. For example, to prepare, you should:

- Know enough about the company to offer at least three things you like and dislike about it.

- Be able to offer three innovative ideas that relate to your position. Do not tell too much, that the company can use your idea and not hire you.

- Think of at least three questions to ask at the end of the interview. Employers really want you to ask something. The best questions are those that show you want to benefit the company or the employer. We know someone who asked the employer what could be done to help her end-of-year review. That made the interviewer laugh, and the applicant got the job.

- Undergo a mock interview with a friend to make sure you sound like yourself and not rehearsed. Make sure your friend asks about your layoff. Some state unemployment offices offer this service. They may even videotape the exercise for you to critique.

THE LAYOFF QUESTION

How do you respond when an interviewer asks how you have been spending your time since your layoff? What should you say when asked to tell something about yourself? Answer both questions in a positive manner. You want to say you have been volunteering or spending your time building your skill set. You never want to criticize a previous employer, no matter the circumstances. If it were a layoff, say so.

If your job was eliminated, say so. These situations are now commonplace. Even if the hiring manager asks what you thought of your previous employer selecting you for elimination, respond in a positive way and state that you understood the manager had to do what was right for the company. All businesses are small. All bosses think your past treatment of managers follows you to the one in front of you.

You will want to ask a timetable and gain a sense of whether the hiring manager will contact you about the new hire. There is nothing more annoying to a hiring manager than when an applicant keeps asking if a decision has been made when he or she clearly said everyone would be notified once a candidate was hired.

POST-INTERVIEW TECHNIQUES

After the interview, remember to send a "thank you" note. In this digital world, emails are acceptable, but a handwritten one stands out more and does not risk being lost in a barrage of daily messages or mistaken for spam. The note should thank the person for his or her time and consideration. Nothing more. You should only contact the hiring manager again if you received permission.

1-7 JOB SEARCH

Are you feeling *it* may happen again? The reality is it may. But you have to focus on your present situation. You should not wait, as most Americans do, until you only have two weeks left of your severance or unemployment benefits. That looming deadline only increases your stress, not to mention your fear of what happens when you do not receive your first check from a new position within two weeks. Realistically, few, if any, hiring decisions are made quickly enough for you to be paid that quickly.

However, let us say you are already past that point. You can still start your search today.

In this section, you will:

● Learn which job search engines are most popular

● Find the sites that could help you in a crunch

● Learn which sites pair job seekers with employers

The quest for a job is difficult enough. We have put the websites and search engines into categories to help you determine which ones are best for you.

Most Popular: Monster.com, CareerBuilder.com, Simplyhired.com and Indeed.com all rank among the biggest search engines that require you to simply type in key words of what you would like to pursue and where you would like to work. There are certainly others, but these are popular on nearly every search and career coach's list.

Carryover/Part-time and Hourly: If it has been a while since you have worked at all and you just need a job —any job — these two sites will help. Snapajob.com is for part-time and hourly jobs. Once you sign up you can type in your zip code and it lists what is available in your area. Allretailjobs.com provides exactly what it sounds like.

Connections: If you want to connect with a recruiter you can sign up at Jobhunt. org. The sign-up process involves setting up a confidential job board and card. It then gives you a dropdown menu for numerous industries. After you make a selection, type in a zip code and the site offers a choice of positions. Voila! You are connected to recruiters of a company with matching criteria. The only down side of this is that it does not cover all of the U.S.

Government: Career One-Stop is the Department of Labor's free service to help you with your search. Learn about job fairs, job banks, and other options. If you attend a job fair, be prepared by asking how many companies are participating. Take 10 or more copies of your resume with you. In case a company representative asks if you have questions, always have at least three ready, but know your time is limited at career fairs. Gauge the conversation and follow the representative's lead. Career One-Stop also offers opportunities to conduct mock interviews before you go, if necessary.

1-8 NEGOTIATING

The idea of going through another layoff or downsizing probably seems absurd, but everyone must prepare for it in these economic times. In this section, you will learn:

- The elements of a great severance package
- The ideal time to request a severance package
- How to avoid a repeat of the pain you are now enduring

REQUEST YOUR SEVERANCE...NOW

FOR YOUR INFO

The best time to request a severance package is when you accept an offer to a new job.

Yes, you read that sentence correctly. The key to success in the event of layoff is to be prepared for it, just as you are prepared for any big money bill such as your mortgage, car payment, or college tuition.

You know the employer wants you and will likely respect you even more for being smart about your future.

Make sure you negotiate the key elements.

DEAL FOR YOUR FUTURE

Think about the things that are the most challenging for you to keep going financially, and you will have no problem negotiating your new severance package. You will want to:

- Keep your health benefits going at the employer's expense as long as possible before COBRA kicks in and you have to pay for it on your own. The higher your title, the longer you are likely to keep this aspect going.

- Negotiate or secure a pay rate that allows you to get paid at the level you expect. Unused holidays or vacation time should also factor into your pay. If you opted to get paid in one lump sum, more taxes would be deducted. Spreading checks across time will help you continue to plan. Make sure all appropriate parties are aware of your terms so if the time comes there will be no lapse in your payments.

- Consider obtaining access to the company's career resources as part of your deal to help you find your next job. Knowing the company will help you secure your next job will eliminate some of your stress.

- Try to get a bonus or stock option if your company typically offers it to every employee each year as a perk or performance-based incentive. If the bonus is only granted at a certain time of year negotiate to get a pro-rated amount no matter when your exit date.

- Get a recommendation letter from the company. Write it yourself if that makes it easier for the person who needs to sign it to understand what you have accomplished. In any case, make sure everyone understands this was negotiated in advance and that you will be leaving the building with at least one — aim for two if you can — recommendation letters.

Once you have a severance package to review have a pro bono employment lawyer review it if you do not understand the language or know how to make sure it is valid.

NEGOTIATING AN OFFER

Once you have an offer, add up all your living expenses, but consider asking for items on the list that the company can pay. Why not a bigger salary? That may not be an option, depending on your years of experience, your latest title, and the size of the company. The more junior your position, the less likely the company is going to budge on negotiating your salary. If you have a higher title, however, ask for a bigger salary, too.

If you cannot get the bigger salary, consider what else you have been working to obtain during your unemployment. For example, maybe you need a new certification. If you ask, your new employer may pay for the training or even a bigger tuition payment than they usually offer. Maybe you have always wanted to attend a conference of leading innovators in your industry, but you could never afford it. Now is the time to request that the company send you to the next one. Maybe you want the right to freelance in a position obviously not a conflict of interest, of course, but are in another division within the company. What a great idea!

Whatever you negotiate, make sure it is documented in your offer letter.

1-9 NETWORKING

So many people do not enjoy networking. The root of the problem is either they do not understand how to do it effectively or they do not know the power of it. Are you in this group? If so, you are not alone.

WHY YOU SHOULD NETWORK

If you have always been a loner one of the most challenging things you will endure during your layoff status is networking. If that is the case for you try to view it as a two-way street in which the vehicles deliver aid. You never know when your expertise or kindness can help the very person who either introduces you to your next boss or gives you that next break or lead.

Networking is all about building relationships, which takes effort, and is a give and take. The goal is to open you up to opportunities that might not have been available otherwise. Another part of networking is reciprocating when you can. Helping others will make them more likely to help you when they can, thus building solid relationships.

In this section, you will learn:

- The essential tools of networking
- The best places to network
- How to achieve the best results

FIND A NETWORK

You may think you have to meet all new people and tell them your story. That is not entirely true.

Friends: Do not avoid your friends who still have jobs. Many of them know you better than you know yourself right now and can offer you job leads accordingly. Friends can also take you as guests to their networking circles and groups. If you make this part of your schedule each week your networking circle will grow. Understand that the more a person sees you the more likely you are to build a rapport. That leads to them remembering you when opportunities arise.

Meetups: Attending a meetup in your area is another way to find unemployed people or others with interests like yours. In Google, if you type "meetup" and key words such as "job," or "unemployed," or "entrepreneur," for your town, you will find the results.

Alumni Organizations: Now is the time to become an active member of your college alumni association. Most are now offering ways to help their alums with career transitions. Why not attend a local meeting and meet the incredible people who will be more than happy to help you simply because you attended the same school? Do not let pride stop you from utilizing this resource. You have no reason to feel shame.

Professional Associations: Remember when you joined that organization related to your field? Your fees are probably still current. Many groups offer a job resource center. Check to see if yours does.

Other Layoff Victims: You should meet with other people who were laid off. Avoid pity parties. You want to remain productive and supportive. Since you are all looking for jobs you can share information. You want to be wary of giving information that could put you in serious competition or in jeopardy, of course. However, if you know a friend wants to work as a manager at a local restaurant, and you know of a position, but have no interest yourself, tell him. He is likely to give you information when you need it.

WHAT EVERY PERSON WHO NETWORKS HAS

Now that you have networking events and places to attend, what do you need to take with you?

Business Cards: In this era of advanced technology, your resume should be posted online somewhere even if it is a simple html format. It is rare for no one to ask for your resume at a networking event, and it is rude for you to offer it to someone on the spot. If you do not have an online resume you can always put your LinkedIn profile URL at the top of your business card. You obviously want to put your name, email, and best phone number. You should list your area of expertise; too, so there is no question what you do. Notice — nothing was mentioned about a layoff or pursuit of a job.

Safe Card Holder: When you give business cards you will certainly want to collect them, too. Have a safe and secure way to do that. Even if you have a card reader on your phone you may opt to record the image of the card later. The last thing you want to do is lose the card of an important contact.

30-Second Elevator Pitch: Tell people the audience you serve, the benefits you bring to the employer, and what sets you apart from others. When you attend networking events you will definitely have a chance to make this pitch. Those who know recruiters looking for your knowledge and expertise will definitely refer you if you entice them and make them want to hear more.

42 ● ● ● ● ● ● ● ● ● ● ● ● ● ● ● ●

ACCOUNTABILITY PARTNERS OR GROUPS

Afraid you will not hold yourself to the discipline of networking as often as you should? You are the perfect candidate for an accountability partner or group. Why do everything alone?

Getting started is easy.

Determine Amount: First, decide if you just want one good friend to help or if you want a small group. Limit your group to six or eight others so everyone has a chance to share information in a relatively short amount of time. Choose people who also need accountability. In short, who else needs accountability, but will be there for you?

Find a Partner or Select Members: For best results, choose people who are unemployed, but be careful to keep details of your conversations confidential. That way you can all feel comfortable to express what you are feeling and experiencing without guilt or repercussion.

Set Rules: Decide what day of the week the group will meet, how often per month, what time, for how long, etc. For best results, gather weekly for 60-90 minutes. You can determine how long each person gets to speak based on the length of your meeting.

Goals Feedback/Success: What do you speak about? Each person should set a specific goal. Yes, everyone wants a job, but you can break that one major goal into several mini ones that you can control. For example, this week one person may want to apply to 30 jobs, attend two networking events, and find one new job lead. Is it feasible for that person? It could depend on his or her other obligations. The group should determine how feedback is to be offered. One of the best feedback processes out there is called the "sandwich" approach used by Toastmasters. Start by saying something positive about the goal. Then list what could be improved and tell why or how another idea may work better. End on a positive note. That way the person does not feel everything he or she says gets a negative response. After all, the last thing anyone wants to hear when unemployed is negativity. In that circumstance, especially, everyone needs to hear something constructive.

You want to begin each meeting with success reports based on goals that have been established. Allow everyone a chance to state objectives they have achieved. Is there a small prize you can give such as chocolate?

New Members: The ultimate pinnacle of success, of course, is when someone achieves their goal of getting a job. That is when he or she is no longer a member of the group and you can opt to bring in a new member. The former member is still a part of your networking circle, which means both circles just got bigger.

1-10 RESUME

Whether you have been out of work for an hour or a year, you may view your resume as a billboard screaming that you are indeed without a job. This section shows you ways to:

● Eliminate the gap of unemployment in a positive way

● Land interviews

● Gain assistance with writing your resume without paying for it

CLOSE THE GAP

A trained hiring manager or recruiter can easily spot an unemployed applicant by looking at their work history. Missing dates show a gap in employment; everybody knows it. That does not mean you should change your dates or lie about it. Instead, use your time wisely to make sure there is no gap.

Certified professional resume writers will tell you that all experience counts. For example, if you volunteer in your field, document it on your resume. Employers only care if you make them money, reduce their costs, and minimize their risks. If you show this as results throughout your resume, including the time you were not with a company, you will shine.

Productive ways to spend your time include:

Learning another language – Do you lack funds for instruction? Perhaps a neighbor or friend speaks the language you want to learn. Remember, most employees need only know a language conversationally.

Taking a business course – Many organizations and the Small Business Association offer classes for free or at minimal cost.

Shadowing someone in your industry – This comes from effective networking. Get someone to allow you to sit with him or her for a couple of hours. Make sure you do not outstay your welcome. If you show enough initiative and expertise when you are there, however, it could lead to a freelance assignment. If you are looking to change careers this is a good way to see if the field is really for you. Afterward, make sure you let the person know how much his or her time is appreciated with a "thank you" card or similar gesture.

Updating your skills — What technology was current the last time you did your resume? If technology passed you by, there are plenty of how-to YouTube videos online and several Meetup groups filled with enthusiasts of various professions involving technology such as photographers, editors, etc. If you are still in contact with the very people who trained you in the first place, ask them to teach you the latest.

THE RESUME FORMAT

With your resume, you have only a few seconds to entice a gatekeeper and/or hiring manager. They are looking for key words from the description and how you can benefit the company. The more you have those two essential elements listed throughout the resume the longer the employer will keep reading. The worst thing you can do is list only the duties you once held.

Instead, your print resume should include:

- Results of your top three efforts since you should have no more than three bullet points per listing.

- An "Areas of Expertise" category to help display your newest skill sets and yes, key words.

- No more than 15 years of experience since age discrimination is alive and well in the corporate arena. If you have more years of work equity, great! No need to bring it up on paper, however, since age discrimination is illegal.

- Your personal email address and phone number. Your home address is not necessary unless you just want to include it. Why would you? Some people like to spotlight the fact that they are local to the area while others prefer to show they are external candidates in many ways. You may also include your LinkedIn address. Regardless, most recruiters will likely search for you on LinkedIn anyway.

You can get free help writing your resume at careeronestop.org, a government agency. There are a number of free templates online, as well. The trick with those, however, is to remember how to write them. Gone are the days of thinking your resume has to be only one page. If you truly have the experience to support it, go for it. Make sure you have a Microsoft Word and PDF version handy to post, as instructed. The Word format should be used only for copying, posting, and updating. The PDF version is for uploading and maintaining a specific format with bullets and any other graphic inserts.

VISUAL ALTERNATIVES

Applicants should always consider that technology and styles change. Stay abreast of — or even ahead of — trends by posting your resume and portfolio on career-oriented websites. Since the paper resume may one day become obsolete, consider video and other innovative ways to display your work history. You can ask a friend who is a videographer to shoot a quality video of you and post it on your YouTube channel and website or rent some equipment at a minimal price and show your own skills. Remember, however, this is one time when both quality and content really matter.

REFERENCES

You no longer put "references available upon request" at the bottom of a resume, but you should always know what your references are going to say. Now it is especially crucial that you have a conversation with your most trusted references so that they understand how you are spending your time and do not focus on your so-called status of being unemployed. If you find people who are uncomfortable with saying what you really are doing, then you do not need to list them. However, you want to pick references that are going to offer a believable report about you. That means they will be able to answer the question about your areas of improvement without harming your chances of getting the job. Again, you should know what your references would say about you. If you cannot agree with them, do not list them. Remember, references are a separate page. If you can get them to recommend you on LinkedIn, too, that is an even bigger victory for you.

SAMPLE RESUME

NAME

Email.address@something.com   (xxx) - xxx-1234

SENIOR ACCOUNTANT

Dynamic Accountant with more than 10 years of combined experience in management and development. Innovative performer with demonstrated record in problem solving. Results-oriented. CPA.

AREAS OF EXPERTISE

Planning | Budgeting | Financial Forecasting | Interdepartmental Collaboration | General Accounting
Process Development | Leadership | Personnel Management & Training | Analysis | Bilingual in Spanish

PROFESSIONAL EXPERIENCE

Madeup Church, Atlanta, GA   2012 – Present
Accounting Consultant
- Analyze reports to increase fundraising efforts by 10% within three months.
- Decrease office costs by 40% within three months by spearheading efforts to brainstorm effective methods.
- Improve and minimize financial risks by training others how to effectively handle basic accounting procedures.

Maximum Financial Group, Atlanta, GA   2005 - 2012
Senior Accountant
- Increased efficiency of office labor by developing plans to minimize input process.
- Trained all new accounting hires to monitor reports three times, resulting in catching more mistakes and saving company more than $500K throughout the years.
- Collaborated with internal departments to develop better protocol to handle vendors, saving time and labor.

Another Accounting Firm, Raleigh, NC   1997 – 2005
Senior Accountant
- Voted Employee of the Month 24 times during tenure for increasing revenue and decreasing costs for as many months.
- Developed financial models for company that are still being used today.

EDUCATION & SPECIAL TRAINING

University of The Best, Atlanta, GA
Bachelor of Science: Accounting
How to Manage Conflict Seminar

OTHER VOLUNTEER ACTIVITIES

Dress for Success

1-11 SOCIAL MEDIA

What is your Klout score? If you are not aware of what Klout is, it is time to boost your social media footprint.

Klout tracks your social media activities and compares your influence in your fields to others.

How would you score professionally?

In this section, you will learn:

- Which social media channels matter for the unemployed
- Which elements grab recruiters' attention and why
- Dos and Don'ts of blogging

THE MOST DISCUSSED CHANNELS

Are you already on LinkedIn, Twitter, and Facebook? If so, that is good news if you are following professional etiquette.

LinkedIn: This is the first place most recruiters look when screening or searching for job applicants. If you do not have a professional photo or complete profile then you have already eliminated yourself from the competition.

You can use the status bar to say you are pursuing a job, but put a professional title under your name. It is of major importance for you to have at least three professional recommendations (no family members, please).

Complete your work history, but if you are in your 40s and older, list only 15 years of experience. Age discrimination and stereotypes are alive and well.

List as many skills as possible that realistically fit you. Do not forget to join LinkedIn groups. Unbelievably, experts suggest about 15 to 20 groups that are relative. Actively participate in forums. Sometimes leads come from them.

The whole purpose of LinkedIn is to connect with other professionals. Increase your circle online by sending invitations to connect through the three degrees of separation you now have. If you do not know someone who is in a position to help you, ask a connection who knows someone to introduce you. Do not use this strategy for recruiters, however. Most hate it. Be smart and build a rapport with someone who knows the recruiter.

Twitter: It is easy to tweet each day about how you have not found a job, if that is the case. Avoid that. Instead, retweet positive messages about tips unemployed people can do. Perhaps tweet some positive feedback you heard about yourself that day while you were volunteering. Remember, a recruiter may want to follow you one day. If he or she reads negativity, you will lose another opportunity. Also, make sure your direct messages are not automatic ones telling the person to follow you on Facebook or some other promotional item. If a recruiter does follow you, that is not a message he or she wants to get.

Facebook: What does your Facebook page say about you? Recruiters and hiring managers have ways to view Facebook profiles, so make sure your photos do not show you drinking or doing anything less than professional. It is okay to have views, but when you are searching for a job you do not have to blatantly show them online. Be careful, too, about friends' comments you allow to show on your page.

Facebook and Department of Labor: There is now a Facebook page you can visit where recruiters and companies post their jobs. If your state is among the top ten with the highest unemployment rate it utilizes the page even more. You can also find tips to improve your skills. That page is facebook.com/socialjobs.

IS BLOGGING ESSENTIAL?

One question that often arises is whether an unemployed person should blog. The simple answer is yes, but here are some tips.

Avoid Badmouthing: You do not want to criticize your previous employer. Potential employers will hopefully read it. If they do, you do not want them to think you are the type to criticize managers who make hard business decisions. No matter what happened in the past, you have to use your energy for good.

Establish Your Credibility: Your blog should pertain to your expertise. You want readers to come to you for advice and your viewpoint. This is really what appeals to hiring managers and recruiters. You will find you know more than you realize. Remember, this area of expertise does not have to relate to your last assignment. Perhaps it is your passion or what you would like to finally pursue.

Proofread: Make sure your blog and your other social media posts are error-free. You want any potential hiring manager to always know you pay attention to details. If copyediting is not your thing use a spellchecker and get a friend who has the expertise to double-check it.

● ● ● ● ● ● ● ● ● ● ● ● ● ● ● ●

1-12 SUCCESS BINDER

Your accountability partner or group, as discussed in the Networking chapter, can also keep track of what is in each person's success binder.

Your meetings can be held with the latest electronic gadgets such as iPads, but you will want hard copies of these documents, too, because you will be asked for most of them. Your accountability partners are the ones to make sure yours are always updated and correct.

As long as your documents are protected, a "binder" can take many forms. These items not only help keep you organized, but they are also needed for your career advancement.

Business Cards/Contacts: This not only means yours, but also those of your contacts. You can find plastic pages for business cards that fit three-ring binders in most office supply or big-box discount stores. Also make space for taking notes about your networking contacts. Did they say to call or email them? When? What happened when you followed up?

Career Solutions: This is the part of your success binder that should change the most. You want to keep track of your progress with each company you pursue. Every step counts. Your group should support your efforts, too, rather than rewarding just "official" successes. Sometimes it takes a lot of courage to make a cold call or finally contact the one place you have always wanted to work. Reward that!

Most Updated Resume: Each time you take a part-time job or volunteer, you should update your resume. You always want to show you are still working, even if it is unpaid.

Bio: Take time to write three paragraphs about yourself that state your inspiration for what you do or want to do, your top three achievements, and your education. Only include personal information such as where you live if it matters to your upcoming position.

References: Always have your list of references and their contact information handy. If you can get each one to send a line or two about you and put them together on one page, even better. You can include this along with your cover letter.

Awards: You should not only include certificates or a list of honors you have earned in your success binder, but also a feasible list of awards you want to earn. If you have chosen a new industry, do your research. This gives you another goal, but you are already an award-winning individual. You can do it again!

Certifications: This is self-explanatory for accomplishments you have already attained. If you continue to train, however, be sure to add new achievements.

Task Force Reports: Are you a member of any task force or committee that relates to your job search? Document this, too.

TIP

Read your binder sometimes. You will be amazed that it is a review of you. Continue to believe that you will have even more success to add to the binder.

WORDS OF WISDOM Throughout the years I have hired people, fired people, and let people go due to layoffs. Letting people go due to layoffs is, by far, one of the most harrowing experiences. I have seen the pain and shock and while I know layoffs are an unpleasant part of many individuals' histories, they are nonetheless part of the journey.

As a hiring manager, I am looking for you to take your journey in stride. In moving beyond this painful experience, I am expecting you to be confident, prepared, and optimistic. In addition to those three attributes, here are my basis tips for success:

1. Do not lose your confidence. So many times I see individuals who are competent, but not confident. It is only when the competence and confidence intersect that you can be most productive and effective.

2. Prepare to be interviewed at any time. You never know when you might meet someone who shows an interest in you and your professional background. Be prepared, because if I ask you to tell me about your background I am expecting that you will have your elevator speech prepared and can recite a brief, concise, and interesting story of your professional journey.

3. Be authentically optimistic and positive. Your job right now is to find a job. Recognize this reality; stay energetic, focused, and positive of your success in finding a job. As a potential employer, I can tell when a candidate is half-heartedly looking for a job. Then I become half-heartedly interested in them. I need to know you are able to stay optimistic and positive in the worst of times.

Sandy Simpson
Director, Enterprise Project Management
Georgia Institute of Technology

Fight another Fight to Dream another Dream

SECTION TWO

FAMILY

Fight another Fight to Dream another Dream

2-1 CHILD CARE

Loss of a job affects the entire family. Termination affects a person economically, emotionally, existentially, socially, and within families.

● Child Care Services

● Head Start

CHILD CARE SERVICES

There are several programs for parents in need of childcare services for dependent children:

- **Child Care Access Means Parents in School Program** — The Child Care Access program supports the participation of low-income parents in postsecondary education by providing campus-based childcare services.

- **Child Care Resource and Referral Services** — Local Child Care Resource and Referral Organizations help parents locate and choose quality childcare by providing referrals to local childcare providers, information on state licensing requirements, availability of childcare subsidies, and other information.

- **Child Care and Development Fund** — The Child Care and Development Fund assists low-income families who need childcare due to work, work-related training, and/or attending school.

- **Child Tax Credit** — The Child Tax Credit program can reduce the Federal tax you owe by $1,000 for each qualifying child under the age of 17.

- **Child and Adult Care Food Program (CACFP)** — The Child and Adult Care Food Program (CACFP) play a vital role in improving the quality of daycare and making it more affordable for many low-income families. The CACFP provides reimbursement for nutritious meals and snacks served to children and adults in daycare facilities. Participants in the program also receive nutrition education materials and training in planning and serving safe, nutritious meals to those in their care.

- **Child and Dependent Care Credit** — The Child and Dependent Care Credit program allows tax reduction by claiming the credit for child and dependent care expenses on your Federal income tax return.

- **Head Start and Early Head Start** — The Head Start program (for children ages 3-5) and Early Head Start program (for pregnant women,

• • • • • • • • • • • • • • •

infants, and toddlers) promote school readiness for children in low-income families by providing comprehensive educational, health, nutritional, and social services.

- **Immunization Grants** – The Vaccines for Children (VFC) program purchases vaccines for children in certain eligibility groups (see below) who cannot afford to buy vaccines. Doctors can get these vaccines for their patients who qualify by joining the VFC program in their state.

- **Indian Child Welfare Act Programs** – The purpose of the programs is to promote the stability and security of American Indian tribes/Alaskan Natives and families by protecting American Indian/Alaskan Native children and preventing the separation of American Indian/Alaskan Native families.

- **Indian Child and Family Education** – The purpose of the program is to begin educating children at an early age through parental involvement to increase high school graduation rates among Indian parents and to encourage life-long learning.

- **Payments for Children of Women Vietnam Veterans Born with Certain Birth Defects** – Biological children of women veterans who served in Vietnam may be eligible for a monetary allowance and possibly vocational training.

- **Social Services Block Grant (SSBG)** – The Social Services Block Grant (SSBG) is a capped entitlement program that provides funds to assist states in delivering social services directed toward the needs of children and adults.

- **Special Education - National Activities - Parent Information Centers** – The Special Education Parent Training and Information (PTI) Centers Program ensures that children with disabilities and parents of children with disabilities receive training and information on their rights and protections under the Individuals with Disabilities Education Act (IDEA) and can effectively participate in planning and decision-making related to early intervention, special education, and transitional services, including the development of Individualized Education Programs (IEPs)

HEAD START

Head Start is a federal program that promotes the school readiness of children ages birth-to-five from low-income families by enhancing their cognitive, social, and emotional development.

2-2 ENERGY

During a job layoff, customer service representatives with every utilities company and for incidentals can be very helpful. When speaking with the respective representatives, be very kind to them. Explain that you are unemployed and looking for financial assistance during this time. In addition, understand the billing cycle, late fees, disconnection schedule, and opportunity to make payment arrangements.

- Energy Programs
- Home Energy Saver
- Energy.gov

ENERGY PROGRAMS

There are three programs to assist during a job layoff:

- **Weatherization Program** — The Weatherization Program is designed to save energy and enhance the self-sufficiency of low-income families by helping you reduce your home heating and cooling bills.

- **Low-Income Home Energy Assistance Program (LIHEAP)** — The Low-Income High Energy Assistance Program (LIHEAP) assists low-income residents with the high cost of home energy. Funding is provided from the Low Income Home Energy Assistance Program (LIHEAP) block grant through the U.S. Department of Health and Human Services.

- **Energy Efficient Mortgage Insurance** — This program helps homebuyers or homeowners save money on utility bills by helping you get loans to cover the cost of adding energy saving features to new or existing housing as part of a Federal Housing Authority insured home purchase or refinanced mortgage.

Also, call your electric company and ask for the name and number for charity organizations in your area that help with payments.

HOME ENERGY SAVER

The Home Energy Saver™ (HES) empowers homeowners and renters to save money, live better, and help the earth by reducing energy use in their homes. HES recommends energy-saving upgrades that are appropriate to the home and make sense for the home's climate and local energy prices. The money invested in these upgrades commonly earns "interest" in the form of energy bill savings, at an annual rate of 20% or more (see examples). HES also estimates the home's carbon footprint and shows how much it can be reduced.

ENERGY.GOV

The Energy Department is working to ensure America's Energy Future, Scientific and Technological Leadership, Nuclear Security, and to resolve the environmental legacy of the cold war. Energy.gov's New Savings Projects provide step-by-step instructions on home energy efficiency improvements. The website subtopics help homeowners save in the following areas:

- Home weatherization
- Windows, doors, and skylights
- Heating and cooling
- Home design and remodeling
- Saving electricity
- Water heating
- Landscaping

2-3 FOOD AND NUTRITION

Food is what the body uses for fuel. Without food the body could not pump blood, breathe, or keep the essential parts of the body in existence. Whether or not you have a family, food and nutrition are essential ingredients to a healthy lifestyle.

- Supplemental Nutrition Assistance Program (SNAP)
- Expanded Food and Nutrition Education Program (EFNEP)
- Meal Programs for Children
- Women, Infants, and Children (WIC)
- Healthy eating on a tight budget

SUPPLEMENTAL NUTRITION ASSISTANCE PROGRAM (SNAP)

Food stamps are officially called the Supplemental Nutrition Assistance Program (SNAP). This federally funded program helps struggling families put food on the table.

EXPANDED FOOD AND NUTRITION EDUCATION PROGRAM (EFNEP)

Families with limited resources may qualify for the Expanded Food and Nutrition Education Program (EFNEP). This federally funded program shows participants how to make a food budget and select nutritious items. EFNEP is designed to assist limited-resource audiences acquiring the knowledge, skills, attitudes, and changed behavior necessary for nutritionally-sound diets and to contribute to their personal development and the improvement of the total family diet and nutritional well-being.

MEAL PROGRAMS FOR CHILDREN

Federally assisted meal programs such as the National School Lunch Program and the School Breakfast Program provide nutritionally balanced, low-cost or free meals to eligible children each school day. Here is a list of the various school meal programs:

- **National School Lunch Program** — The National School Lunch Program

(NSLP) is a federally assisted meal program operating in public and nonprofit private schools and residential childcare institutions. It provides nutritionally balanced, low-cost or free lunches to children each school day.

- **School Breakfast Program** — The School Breakfast Program (SBP) provides cash assistance to States to operate nonprofit breakfast programs in schools and residential childcare institutions. The program is administered at the Federal level by FNS. State education agencies administer the SBP at the State level and local school food authorities operate it in schools.

- **Summer Food Service Program** — The Summer Food Service Program helps to fill the nutrition gap for eligible children when school lets out for the summer.

- **National School Lunch Program** — The National School Lunch Program offers cash reimbursement to help schools serve snacks to children in afterschool activities aimed at promoting the health and well being of children and youth in our communities.

- **Seamless Summer Option** — School Food Authorities (SFAs) participating in the NSLP or SBP are eligible to apply for the Seamless Summer Option.

- **Team Nutrition** — Team Nutrition is an initiative of the USDA Food and Nutrition Service to support the Child Nutrition Programs through training and technical assistance for foodservice, nutrition education for children and their caregivers, and school and community support for healthy eating and physical activity.

- **Fresh Fruit and Vegetable Program** — Free fresh fruits and vegetables in selected low-income elementary schools nationwide.

- **Special Milk Program** — Milk for children who do not have access to other meal programs.

WOMEN, INFANTS, AND CHILDREN (WIC)

Women, Infants, and Children (WIC) provides Federal grants to States for supplemental foods, health care referrals, and nutrition education for low-income pregnant, breastfeeding, and non-breastfeeding postpartum women, and to infants and children up to age five who are found to be at nutritional risk.

HEALTHY EATING ON A TIGHT BUDGET

Food is expensive, but preparing your own meals can be healthier and less expensive than eating out. Get ideas from ChooseMyPlate.gov on how to eat healthy meals on a budget, including:

- Sample 7-day menu
- 30 Ways to stretch your fruit and vegetable budget
- 10 tips for eating better on a budget

2-4 HEALTH CARE

Having health insurance is important because coverage helps people get timely medical care and improves their lives and health. If you had health insurance through your company, it generally will end soon after you are laid off.

- Affordable Care Act
- Medicaid
- Medicare
- Health Insurance for Children: CHIP
- Free vaccines for children
- COBRA: Keeping your insurance if you leave your job
- Healthcare.gov
- Healthfinder.gov
- Medical bills
- Charity care programs
- Emergency Medical Treatment and Labor Act (EMTALA)
- Hill-Burton Free and Reduced-Cost Health Care
- Dental
- Federal Employee Dental and Vision Insurance Program (FEDVIP)

AFFORDABLE CARE ACT

The 2010 Affordable Care Act will reform health insurance, over several years. Some new provisions are already in place; most changes will take effect by 2014. This law holds insurance companies more accountable, expands coverage for young adults, offers small-business tax credits, and provides access to insurance for uninsured Americans with pre-existing conditions.

MEDICAID

States decide on the benefits provided under Medicaid, but Medicaid usually provides health care for low-income children and families, and people with disabilities. Covered services usually include doctor visits, hospital care, vaccinations, prescription drugs, vision, hearing, long-term care, and preventive care for children. Medicaid is health insurance that helps people who cannot afford medical care pay for some or all of their medical bills. Coverage and services vary from state to state.

MEDICARE

Medicare is a government health insurance plan for people 65 or older, people fewer than 65 with certain disabilities, and people with end-stage renal disease. Medicare helps to pay for care in hospitals, skilled nursing facilities, hospice care, and some home health care. Coverage can also include doctors' services and prescription drugs.

HEALTH INSURANCE FOR CHILDREN: CHIP

The Children's Health Insurance Program (CHIP) provides free or low-cost health coverage for low-income children. Each state decides on the benefits provided under CHIP, but all states cover routine check-ups, immunizations, hospital care, dental care, and lab and x-ray services.

FREE VACCINES FOR CHILDREN

Free vaccines are available for children under age 19 who are Medicaid-eligible, uninsured, underinsured, American Indian, or Alaska Native. The Vaccines for Children (VFC) Program helps provide vaccines to children whose parents or guardians may not be able to afford them. This helps ensure that all children have a better chance of getting recommended vaccinations on schedule. These vaccines protect babies, young children, and adolescents from 16 diseases.

COBRA: KEEP YOUR INSURANCE IF YOU LEAVE YOUR JOB

The Consolidated Omnibus Budget Reconciliation Act (COBRA) can help you temporarily keep your health insurance even though you leave your job. Eligibility for the program is based on the reason you left your job; and even if you get to keep your insurance you may be required to pay the entire premium for coverage.

COBRA allows workers and their families who lose their health benefits to choose to continue group health benefits for a limited period at group rates under certain circumstances, such as job loss.

An Employee's Guide to Health Benefits Under COBRA explains your rights to a temporary extension of employer-provided group health coverage, called COBRA continuation coverage.

HEALTHCARE.GOV

Healthcare.gov is a federal government website managed by the U.S. Department of Health & Human Services where you can:

- Find insurance options
- Get help using insurance
- Obtain "The Health Care Law & You"
- Compare care providers
- Locate prevention and wellness

HEALTHFINDER.GOV

Healthfinder.gov is a government web site where you will find information and tools to help you and those you care about stay healthy.

MEDICAL BILLS

Review your medical bills carefully to check for any mistakes. Even if you are covered by insurance, the cost of billing errors may come out of your pocket in the form of higher co-payments and drug costs. After you visit your doctor, your doctor's office submits a bill (also called a claim) to your insurance company. A claim lists the services your doctor provided to you. The insurance company uses the information in the claim to pay your doctor for those services.

When the insurance company pays your doctor it might send you a report called an Explanation of Benefits, or EOB, that shows you what it did. You need to be able to read and understand the EOB to know what your insurance company is paying for, what it is not paying for, and why. An EOB is not a bill.

For Medicare recipients in need of assistance, contact the Centers for Medicare and Medicaid Services (CMS).

There are a number of resources available to individuals who need assistance paying for medical care and prescription drugs:

- State Human/Social Service Agencies offer direct assistance and referrals to other organizations
- State Medicaid Offices help you see if you qualify for assistance
- Local Department of Veterans Affairs (VA) Offices offer programs designed to assist veterans
- Eldercare Locator information specialists put you in contact with resources and programs designed to assist seniors
- State Children's Health Insurance Programs (SCHIP) help insure children of working families who cannot afford health insurance or get it through work
- Benefits.gov allows you to complete a confidential questionnaire and receive a list of programs that may help
- USA.gov Benefits Page provides information on benefits, grants, and financial assistance
- Local Social Security Administration (SSA) Offices assist those on Social Security and Medicare (You may also call the SSA at 1.800.772.1213)
- Disability.gov provides information and resources for people with disabilities
- HealthCare.gov helps you find insurance options, compare care, learn about prevention, and understand the Affordable Care Act

CHARITY CARE PROGRAMS

Charity care programs help uninsured patients who cannot afford to pay their medical bills and do not qualify for government assistance. The patient services department of your hospital can help you find out if you are eligible. If you do not qualify, the hospital may offer you a payment plan.

EMERGENCY MEDICAL TREATMENT AND LABOR ACT (EMTALA)

Under the EMTALA, hospitals receiving Medicare funds must evaluate anyone who comes to the emergency room and requests treatment. If the evaluation confirms that you have an emergency medical condition, including active labor, they are then required to provide stabilizing treatment for you regardless of your ability to pay.

HILL-BURTON FREE AND REDUCED-COST HEALTH CARE

In 1946, Congress passed a law that gave hospitals, nursing homes, and other health facilities grants and loans for construction and modernization. In return, they agreed to provide a reasonable volume of services to persons unable to pay and to make their services available to all persons residing in the facility's area. The program stopped providing funds in 1997, but about 200 healthcare facilities nationwide are still obligated to provide free or reduced-cost care.

DENTAL

The National Institute of Dental and Craniofacial Research (NIDCR), one of the federal government's National Institutes of Health, leads the nation in conducting and supporting research to improve oral health. As a research organization, NIDCR does not provide financial assistance for dental treatment. The following resources, however, may help you find the dental care you need.

Clinical Trials

NIDCR sometimes seeks volunteers with specific dental, oral, and craniofacial conditions to participate in research studies, also known as clinical trials. Researchers may provide study participants with limited free or low-cost dental treatment for the particular condition they are studying.

Dental Schools

Dental schools can be a good source of quality, reduced-cost dental treatment. Most of these teaching facilities have clinics that allow dental students to gain experience-treating patients while providing care at a reduced cost. Experienced, licensed dentists closely supervise the students. Post-graduate and faculty clinics are also available at most schools. Dental hygiene schools may offer supervised, low-cost preventive dental care as part of the training experience for dental hygienists.

Bureau of Primary Health Care

The Bureau of Primary Health Care, a service of the Health Resources and Services Administration (1-888-Ask-HRSA), supports federally-funded community health centers across the country that provide free or reduced-cost health services, including dental care.

FEDERAL EMPLOYEE DENTAL AND VISION INSURANCE PROGRAM (FEDVIP)

The Federal Employee Dental and Vision Insurance Program (FEDVIP) establishes arrangements under which supplemental dental and vision benefits will be made available to Federal employees, retirees, and their dependents. This program allows dental and vision insurance to be purchased on a group basis, which means there are competitive premiums and no pre-existing condition limitations. Premiums for enrolled Federal and Postal employees are withheld from salary on a pre-tax basis.

HOW TO APPEAL A HEALTH INSURANCE CLAIM

TIP

If your health insurer has denied coverage for medical care you received, you have the right to appeal the claim and ask that the company reverse that decision. You can be your own healthcare advocate. Follow these five steps:

1. Review your policy and explanation of benefits

2. Contact your insurer and keep detailed records of your contacts (copies of letters, time and date of conversations)

3. Request documentation from your doctor or employer to support your case

4. Write a formal complaint letter explaining what care was denied and why you are appealing through use of the company's internal review process

5. If the internal appeal is not granted through step four, file a claim with your state's insurance department

2-5 HOME IMPROVEMENTS

Your home is your office while you are looking for a job. It is your address, your identity, and a place where you spend most of the quality time of your life, so it is not surprising this all-important location needs regular maintenance, repairs, and renovations from time to time. Whether you want to fix a faucet or add a new addition to your home, you need to know the facts and the pitfalls of home improvements. Here are some sources that can help:

- Federal loan programs
- Single family housing loans and grants

FEDERAL LOAN PROGRAMS

Rehab a Home with HUD's 203(k)

The Federal Housing Administration (FHA), part of the Department of Housing and Urban Development (HUD), administers various single-family mortgage insurance programs. These programs operate through FHA-approved lending institutions, which submit applications to have the property appraised and have the buyer's credit approved. These lenders fund mortgage loans, which the Department insures. HUD does not make direct loans to help people buy homes.

The Section 203(k) program is the Department's primary program for the rehabilitation and repair of single-family properties. As such, it is an important tool for community and neighborhood revitalization and for expanding homeownership opportunities. Since these are the primary goals of HUD, the Department believes that Section 203(k) is an important program and intends to continue to strongly support the program and lenders that participate in it.

Property Improvement Loan Insurance (Title I)

The Federal Housing Administration (FHA) makes it easier for consumers to obtain affordable home improvement loans by insuring loans made by private lenders to improve properties that meet certain requirements. Lending institutions make loans from their own funds to eligible borrowers to finance these improvements.

Section 184 Indian Home Loan Guarantee Program

The Section 184 Indian Home Loan Guarantee Program is a home mortgage specifically designed for American Indian and Alaska Native families, Alaska Villages, Tribes, or Tribally Designated Housing Entities. Section 184 loans can be used both on and off native lands for new construction, rehabilitation, purchase of an existing home, or refinance.

SINGLE FAMILY HOUSING LOANS AND GRANTS

Single Family Housing Programs provide home ownership opportunities to low- and moderate-income rural Americans through several loan, grant, and loan guarantee programs. The programs also make funding available to individuals to finance vital improvements necessary to make their homes decent, safe, and sanitary. Visit the following sites for information and/or assistance:

- **Rural Housing Guaranteed Loan**
  Applicants for loans may have an income of up to 115% of the median income for the area. Area income limits for this program are here. Families must be without adequate housing, but be able to afford the mortgage payments, including taxes and insurance. In addition, applicants must have reasonable credit histories.

- **Rural Housing Direct Loan**
  Section 502 loans are primarily used to help low-income individuals or household's purchase homes in rural areas. Funds can be used to acquire, build (including funds to purchase and prepare sites and to provide water and sewage facilities), repair, renovate, or relocate a home.

- **Rural Repair and Rehabilitation Loan and Grant**
  The Very Low-Income Housing Repair program provides loans and grants to very low-income homeowners to repair, improve, or modernize their dwellings, or to remove health and safety hazards. Rural Housing Repair and Rehabilitation Grants are funded directly by the Government. A grant is available to dwelling owner/occupant who is 62 years of age or older. Funds may only be used for repairs or improvements to remove health and safety hazards, or to complete repairs to make the dwelling accessible for household members with disabilities.

- **Mutual Self-Help Loans**
  The Section 502 Mutual Self-Help Housing Loan program is used primarily to help very low- and low-income households construct their own homes.

- **Rural Housing Site Loans**
  Rural Housing Site Loans are made to provide financing for the purchase and development of housing sites for low- and moderate-income families.

- **Housing Application Packaging Grants**
  Housing Application Packaging Grants provide government funds to tax-exempt public agencies and private non-profit organizations to package

applications for submission to Housing and Community Facilities Programs.

- **Individual Water and Waste Grants**
  Individual Water and Waste Water Grants provide Government funds to households residing in an area recognized as a colonial before October 1, 1989.

- **Self-Help Technical Assistance Grants**
  To provide Self-Help Technical Assistance Grants to provide financial assistance to qualified nonprofit organizations and public body that will aid needy very low- and low-income individuals and their families to build homes in rural areas by the self-help method. Any State, political subdivision, private or public nonprofit corporation is eligible to apply.

- **Technical and Supervisory Assistance Grants**
  To assist low-income rural families in obtaining adequate housing to meet their family's needs and/or to provide the necessary guidance to promote their continued occupancy of already adequate housing. These objectives will be accomplished through the establishment or support of housing delivery and counseling projects run by eligible applicants.

2-6 HOUSING

Housing is typically the highest line item in a personal household budget. This section will provide direction on various housing situations outlined by USA.gov. Included in this section are:

● Mortgage payment assistance

● Housing assistance: Rent payments

● Facing foreclosure

● Help for the homeless

MORTGAGE PAYMENT ASSISTANCE

Homeowners can lower their monthly mortgage payments and get into more stable loans at today's low rates. For those for whom homeownership is no longer affordable or desirable, the program can provide a way out that avoids foreclosure. Additionally, there are options for unemployed homeowners and homeowners who owe more than their homes are worth. According to USA.gov, there are four main ways to seek mortgage payment assistance:

• **Making Home Affordable** – The Department of Treasury and HUD can help struggling homeowners get mortgage relief through a variety of programs

• **Housing Counseling Agencies** – HUD helps these agencies provide homeowners with free or low-cost advice on home-related issues

• **Housing Relief for Veterans and Servicemembers and to Help More Responsible Homeowners Refinance** – In March 2012, President Obama announced this program to provide relief for servicemembers and veterans as well as support responsible homeowners and the housing recovery

• **Reverse Mortgages** – HUD provides answers to frequently asked questions about reverse mortgages

If you have additional questions about getting mortgage help, contact a housing expert at 888-995-HOPE (4673). These HUD-approved housing counselors will help you understand your options, design a plan to suit your individual situation, and prepare your application. Research shows that homeowners who work with housing experts such as these are more successful and have better long-term outcomes. There is no cost to you for this valuable, around-the-clock service. Help is available in more than 160 languages.

● ● ● ● ● ● ● ● ● ● ● ● ● ● ● ●

TIP

THESE STEPS CAN HELP:

- Do not ignore letters from your lender. If you are having problems making your payments call or write to your lender's loss mitigation department immediately. Explain your situation. Be prepared to provide them with financial information, such as your monthly income and expenses, loan documents/type of mortgage, tax returns, and the amount of equity in your home. Without this information they may not be able to help.

- Stay in your home for now. You may not qualify for assistance if you abandon your property. For example, the Hope for Homeowners program only offers 30-year fixed-rate mortgages to owner-occupiers.

- Contact a HUD-approved housing counseling agency. Call 1-800-569-4287 or TDD 1-800-877-8339 for the housing counseling agency nearest you. These agencies are valuable resources.

HUD counselors frequently have information on services and programs offered by government agencies as well as private and community organizations that could help you. The housing counseling agency may also offer credit counseling. These services are usually free of charge.

HOUSING ASSISTANCE: RENT PAYMENTS

Contact the following agencies to find out what assistance may be available to help with your rent payments:

- Start by contacting your state housing finance agency or local public housing agency office. These organizations may have information about assistance programs administered by your state.

- Contact your local Housing and Urban Development (HUD) office, an excellent resource for information about rental assistance programs, tenant rights in your state, housing counseling, and a number of other programs for groups such as renters, and resources such as public housing.

- If you are a veteran, you may also want to contact the Department of Veterans Affairs (VA). The VA offers many programs designed to assist veterans.

- If you are a senior citizen, you may also want to contact the Eldercare Locator. This is a free service, from the Administration on Aging (AOA) that can connect you with resources and programs designed to assist seniors in your area.

- If you are a rural resident, you may also want to contact the local Rural Development (RD) office. These offices can assist rural residents through the Rural Housing Service.

- If you are a person with a disability, information on housing options is also available.

Finally, to find out what other assistance may be available for you locally, we recommend you contact your state social services agency. Even if you are ineligible for benefits through social services, these agencies may be able to provide referrals to community organizations that might offer assistance. You may also search for and contact community or nonprofit organizations in your area directly for assistance or referral information.

FACING FORECLOSURE

If you miss mortgage payments you may lose your home through foreclosure. Your lender can use foreclosure as a legal means to repossess your home. If you owe more than your property is worth a deficiency judgment is pursued. Both foreclosures and deficiency judgments have a negative impact on your future credit. You should avoid foreclosure if possible.

WARNING

MORTGAGE AND FORECLOSURE SCAMS

Most mortgage professionals are trustworthy and provide a valuable service by allowing families to own a home without saving enough money to buy it outright. However, dishonest or "predatory" lenders do exist and engage in lending practices that increase the chances that a borrower will lose a home to foreclosure. Some abusive practices include:

Leaseback or rent-to-buy scams — You are asked to transfer the title to your home "temporarily" to the scam artist who promises to obtain better financing for your mortgage and allow you to stay in your home as a renter with the option to purchase the home back. However, if you do not comply with the terms of the rent-to-buy agreement, you will lose your money and be evicted like any other tenant.

Fake "government" modification programs — These frauds claim to be affiliated with the government or require that you pay high fees in order

---

to benefit from government modification programs. Remember that you do not have to pay any fees to participate in government-approved programs. Some frauds may even use words such as "federal" or "government-approved" or acquire website names that make consumers think they are associated with the government.

Refinance fraud — The fraud artist offers to be an intermediary between you and your mortgage lender to negotiate a loan modification. They may even instruct you to make payments directly to him or her, which the scammer will send to the lender. However, the fraud artist will not forward the payments to your lender and you could still lose your home.

"Eliminate your debt" claims — Some companies may make false legal claims that you are not required to repay your mortgage or that they know of "secret laws" that can eliminate our debt. Do not believe these claims.

Refinance frauds — You are encouraged to sign "foreclosure rescue" loan documents to refinance your loan. In reality, you have surrendered ownership of your home because the loan documents are actually deed transfer documents. You may falsely believe that your home has been saved from foreclosure until you receive an eviction notice months or even years later.

BEWARE OF FORECLOSURE RESCUE SCAMS — HELP IS FREE

- Beware of anyone who asks you to pay a fee in exchange for a counseling service or modification of a delinquent loan.

- Fraud artists often target homeowners who are struggling to meet their mortgage commitments or are anxious to sell their homes. Recognize and avoid common frauds.

- Beware of people who pressure you to sign papers immediately or who try to convince you that they can save your home if you sign or transfer the deed to your house over to them.

- Do not sign over the deed to your property to any organization or individual unless you are working directly with your mortgage company to forgive your debt.

If you are facing foreclosure get housing counseling and other assistance.

HELP FOR THE HOMELESS

If you are homeless and need assistance contact a homeless assistance agency in your area. The Department of Housing and Urban Development (HUD) and other federal agencies fund programs to help. Local organizations manage these programs and provide a range of services, including providing shelter, food, counseling, and jobs-skills programs.

Veterans
The Department of Veterans Affairs (VA) provides information for homeless veterans.

Families with Children
States are required to have an approved plan for addressing problems with schools. Contact your state Department of Education for more information.

Finding Employment
The Department of Labor (DOL) provides information to help homeless Americans find jobs.

Ending Homelessness
The U.S. Interagency Council on Homelessness (USICH) released the national strategy to prevent and end homelessness, Opening Doors.

2-7 UNEMPLOYMENT BENEFITS

If you have been laid off, you should file for unemployment insurance as soon as possible. The sooner you file, the sooner you can be deemed eligible, and the sooner you can start receiving funds. Unemployment benefit programs pay money to workers who:

- Become unemployed through no fault of their own
- Meet certain other eligibility requirements as determined under state law

You must apply for unemployment benefits through your state unemployment insurance office. Each state has different qualification requirements. NOTE: Even if you received a substantial severance package, you should still file for unemployment compensation.

EXTENDED AND EMERGENCY BENEFITS

Unemployment Insurance Extended Benefits are available to workers who have used up regular unemployment insurance benefits during periods of high unemployment.

Emergency Unemployment Compensation (EUC) offers up to 13 additional weeks of federally-funded unemployment benefits to unemployed individuals nationwide who have already collected all regular state benefits for which they were eligible and who meet other eligibility requirements.

SELF-EMPLOYMENT ASSISTANCE

Self-employment assistance offers unemployed workers the opportunity to create their own jobs by starting their own small businesses. This is a voluntary program offered by individual states. Delaware, Maine, New Jersey, New York, Oregon, and Pennsylvania currently have self-employment assistance programs.

UNEMPLOYMENT BENEFITS AND TAXES

Unemployment insurance benefits are taxable. Any unemployment benefits you receive must be reported as part of your gross income. For more information, visit the Unemployment Compensation website from the Internal Revenue Service (IRS).

WORDS OF WISDOM Time is a valuable commodity that I treasure. As an executive with a wife who is a physician and three children, the process of learning to balance my responsibilities of work, family, and life requires a diligent effort and a life-long journey. A few years ago as I transitioned from the role of a CIO at one company into the same role at another, I had some downtime in between. During that time, without the added stresses of work, I spent time reflecting and uncovered some key points to share.

1. **Reflect**. Reflect on what is important. Our thoughts consumed with work and evening activities give us little time to reflect, and when the weekend arrives we really do not have an opportunity to unwind. Being unemployed gives an opportunity to reflect and see what is important in life. Think about it from a mental, physical, and spiritual perspective. For example, think about how you want to spend time with your family, what you want from your career, and what you want for yourself.

2. **Prioritize**. After you reflect to determine what is important, it is time to prioritize your list. You need to determine what is realistic, when you can make changes, and how to make changes.

3. **Strategize**. Time without a plan leads to a land mine. To avoid going into uncharted territories, think about your career and what you have been doing, what you think you want to do, what is practical, what changes you want to make, and more importantly, what is going to make you truly happy. Once you answer those questions, come up with a strategy to implement.

4. **Implement**. Now that you have a strategy, it is time to implement a daily routine. Create a daily schedule that starts at the normal time you would have gone to work and extends to the time you go to bed. Keep track of your entire day (e.g., people you contacted, time with the family, researching, cooking/cleaning, working out, etc.). Review your daily schedule weekly to see what you have done with your time. Make adjustments to ensure you are spending your time wisely.

5. **Network**. Whether you are working or not working, networking is a key ingredient to building meaningful relationships with others. Become an active networker by keeping in touch with people at least quarterly. You do not need to call each time, but strategically look for resources, tips,

articles, etc., that may interest your network to let them know you are thinking about them. In addition, actively participate on LinkedIn groups, in alumni associations, professional organizations, and religious events.

The above targets are best accomplished when you have a positive attitude. Do not dwell on the "elephant in the room" — that you do not have a job — but rather stay positive and keep yourself honest. Hold yourself accountable for the things you have in your control and do not waste the precious commodity of time.

Salil J. Kulkarni
President and Founder
Vichaar, LLC

SECTION THREE
LIFE

Fight another Fight to Dream another Dream

3-1 CREDIT

Managing credit and debt are major components during a job layoff. Unemployment benefits help supplement the loss of income, but it generally does not cover total monthly expenses, which means your debts may very well overwhelm you. In this section you will learn about:

● Creditors

● Credit reports

● Dealing with debt collectors

● Managing your auto loan

● Credit counseling

● CARD Act Protections for Consumers

CREDITORS

When it comes to debt be proactive. Contact your creditors immediately if you are having trouble making ends meet. Tell them why it is difficult for you. Do not wait until your accounts have been turned over to a debt collector. At that point, your creditors have given up on you. Make arrangements with your creditors is a way that will ease your debt repayments. Draw up a list of your creditors and contact them with a proposal. Inform them that you are experiencing a job layoff. Ask if they have any special programs to assist during this transition period. Ask about the following:

• A debt reduction plan

• An adjusted payment plan

• Extended deferral

• Reduction of the rate of interest

• Reduction in payments

• Forgiving the debt or a portion of it

• Waiving transaction fees

• Crediting your account to lower your bill

• Waiving payments

• Refunding deposits

● ● ● ● ● ● ● ● ● ● ● ● ● ● ● ●

> **TIP**
>
> Do not wait for your creditors to contact you; be proactive before it becomes too late.

CREDIT REPORTS

The Fair Credit Reporting Act (FCRA) requires each of the nationwide consumer reporting companies — Equifax, Experian, and TransUnion — to provide you with a free copy of your credit report, at your request, once every 12 months. The Federal Trade Commission (FTC), the nation's consumer protection agency, has prepared a brochure, "Your Access to Free Credit Reports," explaining your rights under the FCRA and how to order a free annual credit report.

A credit report includes information on where you live, how you pay your bills, and whether you have been sued, arrested, or filed for bankruptcy. Nationwide consumer reporting companies sell the information in your report to creditors, insurers, employers, and other businesses that use it to evaluate your applications for credit, insurance, employment, or renting a home.

You can order your free annual credit report online at annualcreditreport.com, by calling 1-877-322-8228, or by completing the Annual Credit Report Request Form and mailing it to: Annual Credit Report Request Service, P.O. Box 105281, Atlanta, GA 30348-5281.

When you order you will provide your name, address, Social Security number, and date of birth. To verify your identity, you may need to provide some information that only you would know, such as the amount of your monthly mortgage payment.

WARNING PROTECT YOUR CREDIT

Beware: Offers to Skip a Payment
If your credit company invites you to skip a monthly payment without a penalty, it is not doing you a favor. You will still owe finance charges on your unpaid balance. In addition, interest could be adding up on any purchases you make after the due date you skipped.

Beware: Teaser Rates
Some cards are advertised with very low introductory interest rates called teasers. The rate is good for a short period. If you know you can pay what you owe while the low rate is in effect it could be a good deal. However, if the teaser time runs out and you still owe money, you could end up paying a higher rate than you might

WARNING

have without the special introductory rate. Just one late payment could also cancel the teaser rate.

Beware: Credit Insurance

When you take out a loan for a big purchase, a salesperson may try to sell you credit insurance. Your credit card company may also encourage you to purchase credit insurance. The coverage may be promoted as a way for you to protect yourself if your property is damaged or lost. Other credit insurance offers promise to make loan payments if you are laid off, become disabled, or die. It is usually better to buy regular property, life, or disability insurance instead of credit insurance.

Be Alert: 'Credit Repair' Scams

Beware! Many of the benefits promised by fee-based credit repair services are either illegal or things you can do free by yourself. Before you sign up to work with these companies here are some tidbits to keep in mind:

- A credit repair company must give you a copy of the "Consumer Credit File Rights under State and Federal Law" before you sign a contract.

- The company cannot perform any services until you have signed a written contract and completed a three-day waiting period during which time you can cancel the contract without paying any fees.

- The company cannot charge you until it has completed the promised services, according to the Credit Repair Organizations Act.

- It is illegal to erase timely and accurate negative information contained in your credit history.

- Suggestions that you create a new credit history (also called file segregation by requesting an Employer Identification Number from the IRS are also illegal.

- You can work to solve your own credit challenges by requesting a free copy of your credit report and working with creditors to dispute incorrect information.

DEALING WITH DEBT COLLECTORS

The Fair Debt Collection Practices Act is the federal law that dictates how and when a debt collector may contact you. A debt collector may not call you before 8 a.m., after 9 p.m., or while you are at work if the collector knows that your employer does not approve of the calls. Collectors may not harass you, lie, or use unfair practices when they try to collect a debt. In addition, they must honor a written request from you to stop further contact.

MANAGING YOUR AUTO LOAN

Your debts can be unsecured or secured. Secured debts usually are tied to an asset, such as your car for a car loan or your house for a mortgage. If you stop making payments, lenders can repossess your car or foreclose on your house. Unsecured debts are not tied to any asset and include most credit card debt, bills for medical care, signature loans, and debts for other types of services.

Most automobile financing agreements allow a creditor to repossess your car any time you are in default. No notice is required. If your car is repossessed you may have to pay the entire balance due on the loan, as well as towing and storage costs, to get it back. If you cannot do this, the creditor may sell the car. If you see default approaching, you may be better off selling the car yourself and paying off the debt. You will avoid the added costs of repossession and a negative entry on your credit report.

CREDIT COUNSELING

If you are not disciplined enough to create a workable budget and stick to it, cannot work out a repayment plan with your creditors, or cannot keep up with mounting bills, consider contacting a credit counseling organization. Many credit-counseling organizations are nonprofit and work with you to solve your financial problems. However, be aware that, just because an organization says it is "nonprofit" is no guarantee its services are free, affordable, or even legitimate. In fact, some credit counseling organizations charge high fees which may be hidden or urge consumers to make "voluntary" contributions that can cause more debt.

Most credit counselors offer services through local offices, the Internet, or on the telephone. If possible, find an organization that offers in-person counseling. Many universities, military bases, credit unions, housing authorities, and branches of the U.S. Cooperative Extension Service operate nonprofit credit counseling programs. Your financial institution, local consumer protection agency, and friends and family also may be good sources of information and referrals.

Reputable credit counseling organizations can advise you on managing your money and debts, help you develop a budget, and offer free educational materials and workshops. Their counselors are certified and trained in the areas of consumer credit, money and debt management, and budgeting. Counselors discuss your entire financial situation with you and help you develop a personalized plan to solve your money problems. An initial counseling session typically lasts an hour with an offer of follow-up sessions.

The United States Department of Justice has a list of approved credit counseling agencies. For a list of these approved agencies by state and judicial district, select a state, U.S. territory, or commonwealth at http://www.justice.gov/ust/eo/bapcpa/ccde/cc_approved.htm.

WARNING

PROTECT YOURSELF

Be wary of any debt relief organization that:

- Charges fees before settling your debts

- Pressures you to make "voluntary contributions," another name for fees

- Touts a "new government program" to bail out personal credit card debt

- Guarantees it can make your unsecured debt go away

- Tells you to stop communicating with your creditors

- Tells you it can stop all debt collection calls and lawsuits

- Guarantees that your unsecured debts can be paid off for just pennies on the dollar

- Will not send you free information about services it provides without requiring you to provide personal financial information, such as credit card account numbers and balances

- Tries to enroll you in a debt relief program without spending time reviewing your financial situation

- Offers to enroll you in a Debt Modification Plan (DMP) without teaching you budgeting and money management skills

- Demands that you make payments into a DMP before your creditors have accepted you into the program

---

CARD ACT PROTECTIONS FOR CONSUMERS

The Credit Card Accountability Responsibility & Disclosure (CARD) Act brought about sweeping protections for consumers. It limits what your credit card company can and cannot do.

Fees — Credit card companies:

- Cannot change rates or fees without sending you a notice 45 days in advance in most cases.

- Must give you the option of rejecting a fee increase, but be aware that the credit card company may close your account if you reject the fee increase and may require a higher monthly payment.

- Cannot charge you a late payment fee of more than $25, regardless of how much you owe unless one of your last six payments was late or the credit card company can justify a higher fee based on the cost of late payments.

- Cannot charge a late payment fee that is greater than your minimum payment.

- Cannot charge you an inactivity fee for not using your card.

- Cannot charge you more than one fee for a single late payment or any other violation of your cardholder agreement.

- Cannot charge you over-the-limit transaction fees unless you opt in, stating that you want to allow transactions that take you over your credit card limit. If the credit card company allows the transaction without your opt-in, it cannot charge you a fee.

- Can impose only one fee per billing cycle for transactions that take you over your credit limit if you opt in to over-the-limit transactions. You can revoke your opt-in at any time.

Payments — Credit card companies:

- Have to tell you how long it will take to pay off your balance if you make only minimum payments.

- Must mail or deliver your credit card bill at least 21 days before your payment is due.

- Must apply any payments above the minimum required amount to the balance with the highest interest rate, if you have more than one rate.

Interest Rates — Credit card companies:

- Cannot increase your rate for the first 12 months after you open an account unless you have a variable interest rate or an introductory rate; you are more than 60 days late paying your bill; or you are in a workout agreement and do not make payments as arranged.

- Cannot charge higher rates for purchases made before you received notice of a new rate.

- Cannot use the double-cycle bill method when calculating interest; interest can only be charged on balances within the current billing cycle.

- Cannot increase your Annual Percentage Rate (APR) without explaining why it is doing so. If your credit card company increases your APR it generally must re-evaluate that rate increase every six months. Under some circumstances, it may have to reduce your rate after the evaluation.

What's more, a credit card company can grant credit cards to consumers under age 21 only if they can show they are able to make payments or have a cosigner for the card. The Federal Reserve has more information about CARD Act protections.

TIP

GENERAL TIPS

Like everything else you buy, it pays to comparison-shop for credit. For up-to-date interest rate reports on mortgages, auto loans, credit cards, home equity loans, and other banking products, visit bankrate.com. The Equal Credit Opportunity Act protects you when dealing with anyone who regularly offers credit including banks, finance companies, stores, credit card companies, and credit unions. When you apply for credit, a creditor may not:

- Ask about or consider your sex, race, national origin, or religion.

- Ask about your marital status or your spouse unless you are applying for a joint account, relying on your spouse's income, or you live in a community property state (Arizona, California, Idaho, Louisiana, Nevada, New Mexico, Texas, Washington, or Wisconsin).

- Ask about your plans to have or raise children.

- Refuse to consider public assistance income or regularly received alimony or child support.

- Refuse to consider income because of your sex or marital status or because it is from part-time work or retirement benefits.

You have the right to:

- Have credit in your birth name, your first name, and your spouse/partner's last name; or your first name and a combined last name.

- Have a co-signer other than your spouse if one is necessary.

CREDIT

- Keep your own accounts after you change your name or marital status, or retire, unless the creditor has evidence you are unable or unwilling to pay.

- Know why a credit application was rejected. The creditor must give specific reasons or tell you where and how you can get them if you ask within 60 days.

- Have accounts shared with your spouse reported in both your names.

- Know how much it will cost to borrow money.

- OBTAIN A FREE ANNUAL CREDIT REPORT.

For additional information on credit, contact the FTC and the National Consumer Law Center.

3-2 DISABILITY ASSISTANCE

Disability.gov is the federal government website for comprehensive information on disability programs and services in communities nationwide. The site links to more than 14,000 resources from federal, state, and local government agencies, academic institutions and nonprofit organizations. You can find answers to questions about everything from Social Security benefits to employment to affordable and accessible housing.

New information is added daily across 10 main subject areas – Benefits, Civil Rights, Community Life, Education, Emergency Preparedness, Employment, Health, Housing, Technology, and Transportation.

NOTE: Disability.gov is a web portal, which means every time you select a resource you will be directed to another website. For example, a resource about Social Security benefits may direct you to the Social Security Administration's website, ssa.gov. Disability.gov is not responsible for the maintenance of these resources or websites.

PROGRAMS

Disability.gov lists the following 44 programs and a description of each at http://www.benefits.gov/benefits/browse-by-category/category/DIA to assist individuals with disabilities:

- Architectural Barriers Act Enforcement
- Assistance for Indian Children with Severe Disabilities
- Assistance in Puerto Rico, U.S. Virgin Islands, and Guam
- Christopher and Dana Reeve Paralysis Resource Center
- Client Assistance Program (CAP)
- Clothing Allowance
- Coal Mine Workers' Compensation
- Combat-Related Special Compensation (CRSC)
- Disabled Veterans Outreach Program (DVOP)
- Early Intervention Program for Infants and Toddlers with Disabilities
- Federal Retiree Benefits The Office of Personnel Management (OPM)

DISABILITY ASSISTANCE

- Former Worker Medical Screening Program (FWP)
- Independent Living Services for Older Individuals Who Are Blind
- Longshore and Harbor Workers' Compensation
- National Center on Physical Activity and Disability
- National Library Service for the Blind and Physically Handicapped
- National Limb Loss Information Center
- Non-Discrimination in Federally Assisted and Conducted Programs (On the Basis of Disability)
- Protection and Advocacy of Individual Rights
- Social Security Disability Insurance Benefits
- Special Education - National Activities - Parent Information Centers
- Supplemental Security Income (SSI)
- TRIO Student Support Services
- Tax Help for People with Disabilities
- The Energy Employees Occupational Illness Compensation Program Act (EEOICPA)
- The National Emergency Family Registry and Locator System
- VA - Birth Defects Assistance - Health Care - Children of Women Vietnam Veterans Health Care Program
- VA - Birth Defects Assistance - Health Care - Spina Bifida Health Care Program
- VA - Birth Defects Assistance - Payments for Children with Spina Bifida whose Parents Served in Vietnam or Korea
- VA - Birth Defects Assistance - Vocational Training for Children with Spina Bifida or Other Birth Defects
- VA - Grant - Automobiles and Adaptive Equipment for Disabled Veterans and Servicemembers
- VA - Health Care - Basic Medical Benefits Package for Veterans
- VA - Health Care - Domiciliary Care
- VA - Health Care - Home Based Primary Care VA

- VA - Health Care - Nursing Home Care
- VA - Health Care - Respite Care
- VA - Health Care - Services and Aids for Blind Veterans
- VA - Health Care - Veterans Prosthetic Appliances
- VA - Life Insurance - Supplemental Service Disabled Veterans Insurance (Supplemental S-DVI)
- VA - Survivor's Payments - Death Pension
- VA - Veterans Pension for Non-Service-Connected Disability
- VA - Veterans' Compensation for Service-Connected Disabilities
- VA - Vocational Rehabilitation - Vocational Rehabilitation and Employment Services for Veterans with Disabilities
- Vocational Rehabilitation Services Projects for American Indians with Disabilities

OTHER RESOURCES

ADA.gov - Your gateway to information about the Americans with Disabilities Act (ADA). The ADA gives civil rights protections to individuals with disabilities similar to those provided to individuals on the basis of race, color, sex, national origin, age, and religion. Learn more about the ADA and other disability rights laws.

AIDS.gov - An information gateway to guide users to federal HIV/AIDS information and resources on topics including prevention, testing, and treatment and research programs.

Could I Have LUPUS.gov - A federal website dedicated to the autoimmune disease that primarily affects women between ages 15 - 45 years of age. Each year more than 16,000 Americans develop this condition, which can affect various parts of the body, including the skin, joints, heart, lungs, blood, kidneys, and brain. Learn about lupus, its symptoms, treatment options, and available resources.

EyeNote.gov - Provides an application developed by the Bureau of Engraving and Printing for the blind or visually impaired to use as a tool to increase accessibility to U.S. paper currency. It is built for the Apple iOS to allow the user to scan a bank note and communicate its value back to the user. The app is available as a free download on the Apple App Store.

MedlinePlus - A website by the U.S. National Library of Medicine for patients and

• • • • • • • • • • • • • • •

families that provides information about diseases, illnesses, health conditions, and wellness issues. Pages contain links with health information on over 800 topics, as well as information on drugs and supplements, videos, and tools.

President's Committee for People with Intellectual Disabilities (PCPID PCPID works to expand educational opportunities, increase access to technology, improve individual and family support, increase employment and economic independence, and promote access and integration into community life for people with intellectual disabilities.

STOPMedicareFraud.gov - U.S. Departments of Justice and Health and Human Services website that provides information on how to prevent fraud and abuse of the Medicare program. Includes tools such as the Senior Medicare Patrol Program to help older adults volunteer in the fight against Medicare fraud.

Section508.gov - Clearinghouse of information on Section 508 of the Rehabilitation Act, which requires federal agencies to make their electronic and information technology accessible to people with disabilities.

White House Disabilities Web Page - Learn about the Obama Administration's priorities and initiatives as they relate to increasing the employment, community integration, and independence of Americans with disabilities.

3-3 FINANCIAL ASSISTANCE

One of the most difficult things to deal with when unemployed is the loss of income and the feeling of fear when trying to figure out how to pay bills. There are resources to help you and your family cope with financial challenges.

- College students
- Grants and loans
- MyMoney.gov
- Small business loans
- Unclaimed money from the government

COLLEGE STUDENTS

Experiencing a workplace layoff with children is difficult, but when you have a child[ren] in college during your layoff period there are various types of aid. Alternatively, if you have decided to pursue a college degree there are resources available for you.

Grants and Scholarships — Grants and scholarships are often called "gift aid" because they are free money, financial aid that does not have to be repaid. Grants are generally need-based while scholarships are usually merit-based. Grants and scholarships can come from the federal government, your state government, your college or career school, or a private or nonprofit organization. Do your research; apply for any grants or scholarships for which you might be eligible, and be sure to meet application deadlines!

Loans — If you apply for financial aid, you may be offered loans as part of your school's financial aid package. A loan is money you borrow and must pay back with interest. If you decide to take out a loan make sure you understand who is making the loan and its terms and conditions. Student loans can come from the federal government or from private sources such as banks or financial institutions. Loans made by the federal government, called federal student loans, usually offer borrowers lower interest rates and more flexible repayment options than loans from banks or other private sources. The U.S. Department of Education has two federal student loan programs:

- The William D. Ford Federal Direct Loan (Direct Loan) Program is the largest federal student loan program. Under this program, the U.S. Department of Education is your lender. There are four types of Direct Loans available:

❖ Direct Subsidized Loans are loans made to eligible undergraduate students who demonstrate financial need to help cover the costs of higher education at a college or career school.

❖ Direct Unsubsidized Loans are loans made to eligible undergraduate, graduate, and professional students, but in this case, the student does not have to demonstrate financial need to be eligible for the loan.

❖ Direct PLUS Loans are loans made to graduate or professional students and parents of dependent undergraduate students to help pay for education expenses not covered by other financial aid.

❖ Direct Consolidation Loans allow you to combine all of your eligible federal student loans into a single loan with a single loan servicer.

• The Federal Perkins Loan Program is a school-based loan program for undergraduates and graduate students with exceptional financial need. Under this program, the school is the lender.

Learn more about the differences between federal and private student loans at http://studentaid.ed.gov/types/loans/federal-vs-private.

Aid for Military Families — Both the federal government and nonprofit organizations offer money for college to veterans, future military personnel, active duty personnel, and those related to veterans or active duty personnel.

Free Application for Federal Student Aid (FAFSA) — Apply for Federal student aid online using the Department of Education's FAFSA on the Web.

National Student Loan Data System (NSLDS) — The National Student Loan Data System (NSLDS) is a centralized database that stores information on all student loans as well as school enrollment information.

The U.S. Department of Education's Student Aid on the Web — The U.S. Department of Education's Student Aid on the Web is the gateway to Federal student aid. The site offers a single source of free information not only on applying for Federal aid, but on choosing a career, selecting a school, and identifying non-Federal resources to pay for higher education.

U.S Department of Health and Human Services (HHS) Student Assistance Programs — HHS provides a variety of scholarships, loans, and loan repayment programs for students in the health professions, through the Student Assistance Programs of the Health Resources and Services Administration. Visit their website for more information.

Federal Pell Grants — In addition to loans, the U.S. Department of Education provides Pell Grants to students with financial need. Pell Grants do not have to be repaid.

Federal Work-Study — The Federal Work-Study program provides part-time jobs for undergraduate and graduate students with financial need, allowing them to earn money to help pay education expenses. The program encourages community service work and work related to the student's course of study.

Federal Supplemental Educational Opportunity Grant (FSEOG) — A Federal Supplemental Educational Opportunity Grant (FSEOG) is a grant for undergraduate students with exceptional financial needs.

TEACH Grant — A TEACH Grant can help you pay for college if you plan to become a teacher in a high-need field in a low-income area.

Iraq and Afghanistan Service Grants — If your parent or guardian died because of military service in Iraq or Afghanistan you may be eligible for an Iraq and Afghanistan Service Grant.

WARNING

AVOIDING SCAMS

Before you apply for financial aid learn how to spot potential fraud, avoid paying for free services, and prevent identity theft.

Do Not Pay for Help to Find Money for College
Commercial financial aid advice services can cost well over $1,000. You might have heard or seen these claims at seminars, over the phone from telemarketers, or online:

- "Buy now or miss this opportunity." Do not give in to pressure tactics. Remember, the "opportunity" is a chance to pay for information you could find yourself free. Check out our list of free sources of financial aid information below.

- "We guarantee you will get aid." A company could claim it fulfilled its promise if you were offered student loans or a $200 scholarship. Is that worth a fee of $1,000 or more?

- "I have got aid for you; give me your credit card or bank account number." Never give out a credit card or bank account number unless you know the organization you are giving it to be legitimate. You could be putting yourself at risk of identity theft.

● ● ● ● ● ● ● ● ● ● ● ● ● ● ● ● ● ●

> **Do Not Pay for the FAFSA**
> Several websites offer help filing the Free Application for Federal Student Aid
> (FAFSA) for a fee. These sites are not affiliated with or endorsed by the U.S.
> Department of Education. We urge you not to pay these sites for assistance you can
> get free elsewhere. The official FAFSA is at fafsa.gov and you can get free help from:
>
> - The financial aid office at your college or the college(s) you are thinking
>   about attending the FAFSA's online help at fafsa.gov.
>
> - The Federal Student Aid Information Center.
>
> If you are asked for credit card information while filling out the FAFSA online
> you are not at the official government site. Remember, the FAFSA site address has
> .gov in it!

GRANTS AND LOANS

When looking for financial assistance, remember there are differences between
grants and loans. You are required to pay back a loan, often with interest. You
are not required to pay back a grant, but there are very few grants available to
individuals. Most grants are awarded to universities, researchers, cities, states,
counties, and non-profit organizations.

Grants.gov is your source to FIND and APPLY for federal grants. GovLoans.gov
is a partnership of many Federal agencies and organizations with a shared vision:
to provide improved, personalized access to government loan programs. Benefits.
gov lists the following 52 loan/loan repayment opportunities with a description
for each at http://www.benefits.gov/benefits/browse-by-category/category/LOA:

- AIDS Research Loan Repayment Program

- Agricultural Management Assistance Program Agricultural Management
  Assistance (AMA)

- Basic FHA Insured Home Mortgage

- Business Physical Disaster Loans

- Business and Industrial Loans

- Certified Development Company (504) Loan Program

- Clinical Research Loan Repayment Program

- Clinical Research Loan Repayment Program for Individuals from
  Disadvantaged Backgrounds

- Combination Mortgage Insurance for Manufactured Home and Lot
- Contraception and Infertility Research Loan Repayment Program
- Economic Injury Disaster Loans
- Education Consolidation Loans
- Emergency Farm Loans
- Energy Efficient Mortgage Insurance
- Equity Investment - Small Business Investment Company (SBIC) Program
- Extramural Clinical Research Loan Repayment Program for Individuals from Disadvantaged Backgrounds
- FHA PowerSaver Home Energy Retrofit Loan Pilot Program
- Farm Operating Loans (Direct and Guaranteed)
- Farm Ownership Loans (Direct and Guaranteed)
- Farm Storage Facility Loans
- Federal Perkins Loan Program
- Fisheries Finance Program
- Free Application for Federal Student Aid (FAFSA)
- General Research Loan Repayment Program
- Health Disparities Research Loan Repayment Program
- Home Mortgage Insurance for Disaster Victims
- Home Rehabilitation Mortgage Insurance
- Home and Property Disaster Loans
- Indian Health Service Loan Repayment Program
- Indian Home Loan Guarantee Program
- Indian Home Loan Guarantee Program (Section 184)
- Indian Loan Guaranty, Insurance, and Interest Subsidy Program
- Manufactured Home Loan Insurance Federal Housing Administration (FHA)
- Microloan Program

- Military Reservist Economic Injury Disaster Loan Program
- National Health Service Corps Loan Repayment Program
- Nursing Education Loan Repayment Program
- PLUS Parent Loans
- Pediatric Research Loan Repayment Program
- Property Improvement Loan Insurance
- Rural Housing Loans Direct
- Rural Housing: Farm Labor Housing Loans and Grants
- Rural Housing: Housing Repair Loans and Grants
- Short Term Lending Program
- Stafford Loans for Students
- VA - Home Loan - Construction
- VA - Home Loans - Cash Out Refinance (Regular Refinance)
- VA - Home Loans - Interest Rate Reduction Refinancing Loan
- VA - Home Loans - Native American Direct Loan (NADL) Program
- VA - Home Loans - Regular Purchase
- VA - Life Insurance - Veterans Life Insurance Policy Loans

MYMONEY.GOV

 FOR YOUR INFO MyMoney.gov is the U.S. government's website dedicated to teaching all Americans the basics about financial education.

Whether you are buying a home, balancing your checkbook, or investing in your 401(k), the resources on MyMoney.gov can help you maximize your financial decisions. Throughout the site, you will find important information from 20 Federal agencies and Bureaus designed to help you make smart financial choices. On the MyMoney.gov at http://www.mymoney.gov/category/topic1/starting/-losing-job.html you can find valuable resources related to starting and/or losing a job:

Saving Matters Video — Many workers do not realize how important it is to get an early start on saving for retirement. This Department of Labor Employee Benefits Security Administration video provides information for workers about the importance of saving for retirement and how to get started. The video also has links to additional online tools to help workers take full advantage of their employer-sponsored benefits.

Know Your Health Benefit Rights Video — Many workers are not aware of the laws that protect their health benefits. This Department of Labor Employee Benefits Security Administration video provides information for workers about their healthcare rights. The video also has links to additional information to help workers take full advantage of their employer-sponsored benefits.

Success Stories: Reaching Households Struggling to Survive a Job Loss or Wage Reduction — "Money Smart News Success Stories," the FDIC's quarterly online newsletter, provides updates on the Money Smart program and highlights success stories from those using Money Smart.

New Employee Savings Tips - "Time Is On Your Side" — If you are starting a new job, this publication provides tips to help you save for your long-term goals in addition to your short-term goals. If you start saving now the money will have years to grow and you will have a better chance of being able to do all the things you want to do in the future. In addition, by starting early you will need to save a lot less later on.

Work Changes Require Health Choices, Protect Your Rights — Opportunities and setbacks are part of life, especially when it comes to work. That is why it is important to know how changes in employment status can affect health coverage. Whether you have landed a new job, lost or retired from one, or you are thinking about changing employers, find out today how to have the health benefits you might need tomorrow. Know your rights. Exercise your options.

Protecting Your Pension and Health Benefits after Job Loss — Job termination or a reduction in hours can result in a loss of retirement and health benefits. However, employees and their families may have rights under Federal law that can help protect benefits when employment changes. This publication provides information on the laws that protect your benefits when facing job loss and where you can go for further information.

Disaster Unemployment Assistance — Disaster Unemployment Assistance provides financial assistance to individuals whose employment or self-employment has been lost or interrupted as a direct result of a major disaster and who are not eligible for regular unemployment insurance benefits.

Out of Work? How to Deal with Creditors — If you have recently lost your job, your first thought may be, "How will I make ends meet?" The Federal Trade Commission spells out your rights when it comes to fair debt collection and credit reporting practices.

Health and Retirement Benefits after Job Loss Toolkit — Job termination or reduction in hours can result in loss of retirement and health benefits. However, employees and their families may have rights under Federal law that can help protect benefits when employment changes. This toolkit provides many resources to help employees facing job loss or reduction in hours with information about their benefit rights to help them make informed decisions. Many of the materials included on this page are available in Spanish.

Retirement and Health Care Coverage — Questions & Answers for Dislocated Workers; important information for workers who have lost their jobs about protecting their retirement and health benefits to help them make informed decisions.

SMALL BUSINESS LOANS

Most small businesses rely on lenders to provide the capital they need to either open a business or to finance capital improvements. Without loans, many small business owners would be unable to realize their dreams of opening a business or expanding their operations. When you experience a workplace layoff instead of waiting for a new employer to hire you or your previous employer to rehire you explore your options as a small business owner.

Small Business Administration (SBA)'s Role — Even though SBA does not loan money directly to small business owners they may play an important role for people who want to finance or grow their businesses. When you apply for a SBA-backed loan at your local bank or credit union you are asking SBA to provide a guarantee that you will repay your loan as promised.

Small Business Administration (SBA) Loan Programs — SBA offers a variety of loan programs for very specific purposes. Take some time to study the programs described in this section to see if you qualify to participate.

Small Business Administration (SBA) Disaster Loans — SBA provides low-interest disaster loans to homeowners, renters, businesses of all sizes, and private, nonprofit organizations to repair or replace real estate, personal property, machinery & equipment, inventory, and business assets that have been damaged or destroyed in a declared disaster.

How to Prepare Your Loan Application — Each SBA loan program has its own eligibility criteria and application process. However, as you prepare to submit your paperwork you will need to gather and prepare similar loan application documentation.

Find Small Business Loans — Federal, state, and local governments offer a wide range of financing programs to help small businesses start and grow their operations. These programs include low-interest loans, venture capital, and scientific and economic development grants.

UNCLAIMED MONEY FROM THE GOVERNMENT

Check unclaimed property, credit unions, mortgage refunds, and more.

- Bank Failures
- Credit Union Unclaimed Shares
- Damaged Money
- Get Your Money Back – "Investors Claims Funds" and Class Actions
- HUD/FHA Mortgage Insurance Refunds
- Pension Funds from Former Employers
- Savings Bonds Calculator
- Savings Bonds Interest
- Savings Bonds Recovery
- States' Unclaimed Property
- Treasury Hunt

3-4 GOVERNMENT AGENCIES

It is important to understand which government agencies can be helpful to you during a job layoff. Take advantage of this opportunity to visit agency websites to learn more about services, benefits, and opportunities for which you may be eligible to apply during you layoff period.

FEDERAL EXECUTIVE DEPARTMENTS

Department of Education (ED) – The Department of Education establishes policy for the nation's schools, and administers and coordinates most federal education assistance.

Department of Health and Human Services (HHS) – The Department of Health and Human Services is the United States government's principal agency for protecting the health of all Americans and providing essential human services.

Department of Housing and Urban Development (HUD) – The Department of Housing and Urban Development oversees homes owned by the government and ensures that tenants and renters are treated fairly under the law.

Department of Labor (DOL) – The Department of Labor supports the workforce by improving working conditions, and protecting employee benefits.

STATE GOVERNMENTS

Visit the government website for each state, the District of Columbia, and U.S. territories and associated states to learn about additional benefits.

LOCAL GOVERNMENTS

Locate resources and websites on U.S. cities and local governments to learn about additional benefits.

TRIBAL GOVERNMENT

Visit tribal government websites to learn about additional benefits.

3-5 LEGAL ASSISTANCE

During a job layoff there may come a time when you need legal assistance and do not have the financial resources to pay. Legal Services Corporation (LSC) is the single largest funder of civil legal aid for low-income Americans in the nation. Established in 1974, LSC operates as an independent 501(c) (3) nonprofit corporation that promotes equal access to justice and provides grants for high-quality civil legal assistance to low-income Americans. LSC distributes more than 90 percent of its total funding to 134 independent nonprofit legal aid programs with more than 900 offices.

LSC promotes equal access to justice by awarding grants to legal services providers through a competitive grants process; conducting compliance reviews and program visits to oversee program quality and compliance with statutory and regulatory requirements as well as restrictions that accompany LSC funding; and by providing training and technical assistance to programs. LSC encourages programs to leverage limited resources by collaborating with other funders of civil legal aid, including state and local governments, Interest on Lawyers' Trust Accounts (IOLTA), access to justice commissions, the private bar, philanthropic foundations, and the business community.

A bipartisan board of directors whose 11 members are appointed by the President and confirmed by the Senate heads the Corporation.

Legal assistance is necessary to address many issues that affect low-income individuals and families. The most frequent cases involve:

> **Family law** – LSC grantees help victims of domestic violence by obtaining protective and restraining orders, help parents obtain and keep custody of their children, assist family members in obtaining guardianship for children without parents, and other family law matters. More than a third of all cases closed by local LSC programs are family law cases.

> **Housing and Foreclosure Cases** – As the second largest category of all cases closed, these matters involve helping to resolve landlord-tenant disputes, helping homeowners prevent foreclosures or renegotiate their loans, assisting renters with eviction notices whose landlords are being foreclosed on, and helping people maintain federal housing subsidies when appropriate.

> **Consumer Issues** – Nearly 12 percent of cases involve protecting the elderly and other vulnerable groups from being victimized by

unscrupulous lenders, helping people file for bankruptcy when appropriate, and helping people manage their debts.

Income Maintenance — More than 12 percent of cases involve helping working Americans obtain promised compensation from private employers and helping people obtain and retain government benefits such as disability benefits to which they are entitled.

Helping Military Families — StatesideLegal.org is the first website in the nation to focus exclusively on federal legal rights and legal resources important to veterans and is funded by an LSC Technology Initiatives Grant. This free service enables military families and veterans to access a wide array of legal information and assistance. The Department of Veterans Affairs, in a directive, encourages use of the website in connection with service to homeless veterans.

Responding to Disasters — LSC has a long history with helping victims of natural disasters. LSC has built a national network of experience and expertise including legal services providers and national organizations such as the American Red Cross and Federal Emergency Management Agency (FEMA) to help programs better serve victims when disasters strike.

To find legal aid by state and county, visit http://lsc.gov/find-legal-aid.

3-6 SENIOR CITIZENS

With the nation's unemployment rate hovering around 9% on average — and even higher in past months — the number of seniors becoming unemployed is higher than ever.

- AARP Foundation
- Government resources
- Housing for seniors

AARP FOUNDATION

For many Americans age 50 and older a single event — a lost job, a health crisis, the loss of a spouse or partner — can quickly lead to catastrophic circumstances on many fronts. The AARP Foundation has identified four interrelated priority areas where they can have the greatest impact: hunger, income, housing, and isolation. This work is supported by a longstanding commitment to legal advocacy on behalf of older Americans everywhere.

The AARP Foundation is also working side-by-side with hardworking, trusted organizations in communities across the nation. These organizations are doing a heroic job of helping struggling Americans, but with the numbers of people in crisis growing every day it is a challenge to reach everyone and ensure that those who need support know where to find it. The AARP Foundation has a powerful multiplier effect for much-needed programs and services to reach more people and make resources go further.

- Hunger
- Income
- Housing
- Isolation
- Legal Advocacy

GOVERNMENT RESOURCES

Find government resources for seniors on money, housing, health, consumer protection, and more.

Education, Jobs, and Volunteerism for Seniors — Most people will spend up to 1/3 of their life in retirement, depending on the age at which they choose to stop working full-time. Research has shown that staying engaged during retirement can result in better health and prolonged life. Some of the ways satisfied retirees stay engaged are through education, part-time work, and volunteering.

Health for Seniors — Find doctors and healthcare facilities, get Medicare and Medicaid resources, look up information about prescription drugs, and more.

Laws and Regulations Concerning Seniors — Learn about the Age Discrimination in Employment Act, the Older Americans Act, the Social Security Act, and more.

Money and Taxes for Seniors — Get tax tips for seniors, learn about CDs and other ways of saving money, and more.

Retirement — Use these resources to help you estimate your retirement benefits, learn about factors that could affect your retirement, and more.

HOUSING FOR SENIORS

Learn about reverse mortgages, look into eldercare at home, compare nursing homes, and more.

Administration on Aging - Housing — AoA, through the Older Americans Act and other legislation, supports programs that help older adults maintain their independence and dignity in their homes and communities.

American Association of Homes and Services for the Aging — LeadingAge's Consumer Hub offers information and support to help people make the most of the aging experience. This includes a directory of not-for-profit organizations committed to meeting people's needs and preferences as they age.

Eldercare Locator — The Eldercare Locator, a public service of the Administration on Aging, U.S. Department of Health and Human Services, is a nationwide service that connects older Americans and their caregivers with information on senior services.

Home Equity Advisor — Find information, tools, and consumer advice on using and protecting the value in your home. Get custom advice for your life situation even if you need help now. Created by the nonprofit National Council on Aging and made possible by a generous grant from the FINRA Investor Education Foundation.

Housing Information for Seniors — Looking for housing options for you, an aging parent, relative, or friend? Do some research first to determine what kind of assistance or living arrangement you need, what your health insurance might cover, and what you can afford.

Reverse Mortgages for Seniors — Reverse mortgages are becoming popular in America. Reverse mortgages are a special type of home loan that lets a homeowner convert the equity in his/her home into cash. They can give older Americans greater financial security to supplement social security, meet unexpected medical expenses, make home improvements, and more.

3-7 UNITED WAY

United Way Worldwide is the leadership and support organization for a network of nearly 1,800 community-based organizations in 45 countries and territories. To advance the common good and mobilize the caring power of communities around the world, United Way seeks to:

- Ignite a worldwide social movement, and thereby mobilize millions to action to give, advocate, and volunteer

- Galvanize and connect all sectors of society — individuals, businesses, non-profit organizations, and governments — to create long-term social change that produces healthy, well-educated, and financially-stable individuals and families

- Raise, invest, and leverage billions of dollars annually in philanthropic contributions to create and support innovative programs and approaches to generate sustained impact in local communities

- Hold themselves accountable to this cause through steadfast commitment to continually measure — in real terms — improvements in education, income and health

During your job layoff you can contact the United Way to find support in the following areas:

- Business/Consumer/Environmental Services
- Clothing/Food/Personal Goods/Services
- Counseling/Crisis Services
- Disaster Services
- Education/Training
- Employment Assistance/Services
- Facility Types
- Family/Community Services
- Financial Services/Assistance
- Health/Medical/Mental Health
- Holiday Assistance/Toys for Tots

- Information Services
- Legal Services/Immigration
- Military Personnel
- Shelter/Housing
- Transportation Services/Assistance

To learn more about the United Way, visit http://www.unitedway.org/. To find your local United Way office, visit http://apps.unitedway.org/myuw/.

3-8 VETERANS

Veterans of the United States armed forces may be eligible for a broad range of benefits and services provided by the U.S. Department of Veterans Affairs (VA). These benefits are legislated in Title 38 of the United States Code.

Eligibility for most VA benefits is based upon discharge from active military service under other than dishonorable conditions. Active service means full-time service other than active duty for training as a member of the Army, Navy, Air Force, Marine Corps, Coast Guard, or as a commissioned officer of the Public Health Service, Environmental Science Services Administration, or National Oceanic and Atmospheric Administration or its predecessor, the Coast and Geodetic Survey. Generally, men and women veterans with similar service may be entitled to the same VA benefits.

- Benefits for Veterans
- Education for Veterans
- Health Care for Veterans
- Job Resources for Veterans
- Returning Service Members
- Women Veterans
- Vocational Rehabilitation and Employment (VR&E)

BENEFITS FOR VETERANS

eBenefits.va.gov is a portal; a central location for Veterans, Service Members, and their families to research, find, access, and in time, manage their benefits and personal information. Find benefits by state or topic, such as health, employment, education, and more.

EDUCATION FOR VETERANS

The Department of Veterans Affairs administers a variety of education benefit programs. Many veterans and active duty personnel can qualify for more than one education benefits program, including:

- The Post-9/11 GI Bill

- Montgomery GI Bill - Active Duty (MGIB-AD)
- Montgomery GI Bill - Selected Reserve (MGIB-SR)
- Reserve Educational Assistance Program (REAP)
- Veterans Educational Assistance Program (VEAP)
- Educational Assistance Test Program (Section 901)
- Survivors' and Dependents' Educational Assistance Program (DEA)
- National Call to Service Program
- Veterans Retraining Assistance Program
- Free education and vocational counseling services

HEALTHCARE FOR VETERANS

If you served in the active military, naval, or air service and are separated under any condition other than dishonorable, you may qualify for VA healthcare benefits. Find the care you need or learn more about health programs and how you can protect your health.

JOB RESOURCES FOR VETERANS

Browse the job bank at Vetsuccess.gov and get job tools and tips. There are four easy ways to search for a job.

RETURNING SERVICE MEMBERS

Have you recently returned from military service? Here are just a few of the programs the VA offers:

5 Years of Cost Free Health Care — OEF/OIF combat veterans can receive cost-free medical care for any condition related to their service in the Iraq/Afghanistan theater for five years after the date of their discharge or release.

180 Day Dental Benefit — OEF/OIF combat veterans may be eligible for one-time dental care, but must apply within 180 days of separation date from active duty.

Find Family Support at Vet Centers — If you have served in ANY combat zone, local Vet Centers can help you and your family with free readjustment counseling and outreach services.

Going Back to School — the VA pays benefits to eligible veterans, reservists, and active duty service members to support continuing education goals, including on-the-job training, apprenticeships, and non-college degree programs.

Finding a Job — You served your country; now you are ready for a new challenge. What do you want to do next? Get help finding and securing a job, browse career opportunities, or learn more about working at the VA.

How Do I Get Help — Am I eligible? VA regional offices can help you with completing and filing the right VA forms.

WOMEN VETERANS

In November 1994, Public Law 103-446 established the Center for Women to monitor and coordinate the VA's administration of healthcare and benefit services and programs for women veterans. The Center serves as an advocate for a cultural transformation (both within VA and in the general public) in recognizing the service and contributions of women veterans and women in the military, and in raising awareness of the responsibility to treat women veterans with dignity and respect. The Director, Center for Women Veterans, acts as the primary advisor to the Secretary of Veterans Affairs on all matters related to policies, legislation, programs, issues, and initiatives affecting women veterans. Visit va.gov to learn more about healthcare and benefit programs for women.

VOCATIONAL REHABILITATION AND EMPLOYMENT PROGRAM (VR&E)

The Vocational Rehabilitation and Employment (VR&E) VetSuccess Program is authorized by Congress under Title 38, Code of Federal Regulations, Chapter 31. It is sometimes referred to as the Chapter 31 program. The VetSuccess program assists veterans with service-connected disabilities to prepare for, find, and keep suitable jobs. For veterans with service-connected disabilities so severe they cannot immediately consider work, VetSuccess offers services to improve their ability to live as independently as possible.

Services that may be provided by the VR&E VetSuccess Program include:

- Comprehensive rehabilitation evaluation to determine abilities, skills, and interests for employment
- Vocational counseling and rehabilitation planning for employment services
- Employment services such as job training, job-seeking skills, resume development, and other work readiness assistance
- Assistance finding and keeping a job, including the use of special employer incentives and job accommodations
- On-the-Job Training (OJT), apprenticeships, and non-paid work experiences
- Post-secondary training at a college, vocational, technical, or business school
- Supportive rehabilitation services including case management, counseling, and medical referrals
- Independent living services for veterans unable to work due to the severity of their disabilities

3-9 VITAL RECORDS

Vital records are records of life events kept under governmental authority, including birth certificates, marriage licenses, divorce records, and death certificates. In some jurisdictions, vital records may also include records of civil unions or domestic partnerships. When applying for benefits from various organizations and non-profit agencies, often you will need to provide documentation.

To access your individual state and territory for ordering information, visit http://www.cdc.gov/nchs/w2w.htm. To use this valuable tool you must first determine the state or area where the birth, death, marriage, or divorce occurred, then click on that state or area. Please follow the provided guidelines to ensure an accurate response to your request.

The federal government does not distribute certificates, files, or indexes without identifying information for vital records. Applications for passports can be obtained through the U.S. State Department at http://travel.state.gov/passport/passport_1738.html. Family issues such as marriage, divorce, death, and birth abroad can be found at http://travel.state.gov/law/family_issues/family_issues_601.html.

REPLACE YOUR VITAL DOCUMENTS

Fortunately, you can replace most important personal records.

Address Change - When you move be sure to change your address with the Post Office, IRS, and other government agencies so that you will continue to receive mail and any government benefits at your new location.

Bank Records - Get financial tips and resources for disaster recovery.

Birth, Marriage, and Death Certificates - Get records based on the location of the birth, death, marriage, or divorce.

Damaged Money - The Treasury Department will exchange mutilated or damaged U.S. currency.

Document Restoration: Fire - The Library of Congress offers information on restoring fire-damaged documents and collections.

Document Restoration: Flood - The National Archives offers information on how to care for flood-damaged photos, books, papers, and more.

Drivers' Licenses and Vehicle Registrations – Find your state's motor vehicle department to get or replace your driver's license and to register your car.

Federal Civilian Personnel Records – Go to the National Archives website for guidance on requesting personnel records for former federal civilian employees. Current federal workers can get personnel records from your human resources office.

Green Card Replacement – Get instructions on how to replace a lost, stolen, or damaged permanent resident card (green card).

Medicare Card Replacement – Learn how to replace a lost, stolen, or damaged Medicare card.

Military Service Records – Get copies of military service records as proof of military service or to research genealogy.

Passport – Report a lost or stolen passport immediately. Contact the nearest U.S. embassy or consulate if your passport is lost or stolen overseas.

Savings Bonds Recovery – Cash and replace lost, stolen, or destroyed bonds.

School Records – Contact your former school or the appropriate school district if the school has closed.

Social Security Card Replacement – Learn how to replace your lost or stolen Social Security card.

Tax Return – Request a copy of your federal tax return from the Internal Revenue Service (IRS).

3-10 VOLUNTEERING

Volunteer work is important for your health. The Corporation for National and Community Service says that volunteering improves psychological and physical health. Volunteers reap the benefits of feeling a personal sense of accomplishment while building social networks that, in turn, support them in times of stress.

Volunteer work is also an important part of your resume. A history of volunteering demonstrates your commitment to the community and a willingness to work for the betterment of others.

At a time when many Americans are struggling with the loss of jobs or homes you can help meet some of the most basic needs by working to reduce hunger, secure donated clothing, and strengthen community resources. Here are some areas to explore:

● Volunteering in America

● United We Serve

● Volunteer.gov

● Take Pride in America

VOLUNTEERING IN AMERICA

Volunteers are resolute in their commitments to serving their neighbors and communities with 62.8 million adults volunteering almost 8.1 billion hours in local and national organizations in 2010, services valued at almost $173 billion. Explore the Volunteering in America website for the most comprehensive data on volunteering ever assembled including volunteer profiles for all 50 states and the District of Columbia as well as hundreds of metropolitan areas, rankings, demographic trends, and profiles of volunteer organizations making an impact on some of our nation's toughest challenges.

UNITED WE SERVE

United We Serve is a nationwide service initiative that helps meet growing social needs resulting from the economic downturn. With the knowledge that ordinary people can achieve extraordinary things when given the proper tools, President Obama is asking us to come together to help lay a new foundation for growth. This initiative aims both to expand the impact of existing organizations by engaging new volunteers in their work and to encourage volunteers to develop their own "do-it-yourself" projects.

The President has said that the challenges America faces are unprecedented and that we need to build a new foundation for economic growth in America. The Administration has begun this work with dramatic new investments in education, healthcare, and clean energy, but those in government cannot do it alone. Economic recovery is as much about what communities are doing as what Washington is doing. It will take all of us working together.

United We Serve encourages all Americans to volunteer in their communities. Serve.gov is an online resource for not only finding volunteer opportunities in your community, but also creating your own. Use Serve.gov to help you do your part. America's foundation will be built one community at a time and it starts with you.

VOLUNTEER.GOV

Volunteer.gov is America's Natural and Cultural Resources Volunteer Portal.

TAKE PRIDE IN AMERICA

Take Pride in America is a nationwide partnership program authorized by Congress to promote the appreciation and stewardship of our nation's public lands. The Take Pride in America program is administered by the U.S. Department of the Interior for the benefit of all public lands at all levels of government nationwide.

In addition to promoting public lands stewardship, Take Pride in America recognizes and honors outstanding volunteers through its annual national awards ceremony. Individuals, groups, organizations, programs, and federal land managers are honored for their contributions to our public lands and for their efforts in utilizing volunteers in creative and innovative ways.

In support of President Obama and Secretary Ken Salazar's call to service, Take Pride in America is leading the U.S. Department of the Interior's United We Serve initiative.

"Life is what happens while you are planning something else."

WORDS OF WISDOM Not many people plan to lose their jobs. Even if a job loss is anticipated the actual event can be very unsettling. I have lost jobs three times in my career due to company cutbacks. You really do not get used to it; however, it does not have to be the end of the line or the demise of a career. There are three things I recommend that have worked for me when I have been out of a job:

- Allow yourself 15 minutes of ranting and raving; then get over it. It is a poor use of your energy.

- Take stock of yourself. Do a personal inventory, noting your strengths and weaknesses. If you do not know how there are plenty of helpful web sites out there to help you.

- Work your network as hard as you can, but do not ask for a job; ask people to talk to who might know about a job. In 2005, I had roughly 35 contacts on LinkedIn. I now have over 500. The message: never stop networking.

Every job I ever held since I graduated from college came from my network. There is a misconception that only extroverts are good at networking. Not true. Anyone can network if they approach it the right way. In this day, with all the modern technologies available, it is much easier to network than 30 years ago. Start with friends, family, acquaintances, business associates, and build from there. Most folks will want to help so long as you do not put them on the spot.

Remember this: you have a lot to offer and losing your job does not reduce your strengths, which are what you build upon as you look for your next job. I have had outplacement people tell me to treat the job hunt as a new and exciting time in your life. What they are really saying is work hard on maintaining a positive attitude. If you are down, it will show. Celebrate all achievements, big or small; e.g. getting an interview, getting to talk to someone who might know someone who might have a job that is a perfect fit for you.

What you want is out there, but it is up to you to find it.

Wally Weihe, President
Wallace Weihe & Associates
WeiheAssociates.com

APPENDICES

Fight another Fight to Dream another Dream

APPENDIX 1 — TIPS

OTHER SOURCES OF INCOME

Time is of the essence when trying to make your housing payments. Many of the government programs take months before closing. Therefore, you may need alternatives to help pay your housing expenses while you wait. Here are a few alternatives:

- Babysitting
- Cleaning houses
- Collecting aluminum cans
- Driving people to the airport
- Family assistance
- Freelance writing
- House-sitting
- Lawn care
- Liquidating assets
- Part-time work
- Pet-sitting
- Playing music in church or at weddings
- Renting out a room
- Renting out your truck or van
- Starting an online store
- Teaching English to adults
- Tutoring
- Walking dogs
- Writing an eBook

GOVERNMENT BENEFITS

Benefits.gov (formerly GovBenefits.gov) was launched in an effort to provide citizens with easy, online access to government benefits and assistance programs. Benefits.gov can help you identify grants, loans, financial aid, and other benefits from the U.S. government for which you may be eligible and tell you how and where to apply. Benefits.gov offers multiple search methods to help you quickly find benefits based on the type of assistance you are interested in through its Benefit Finder.

What is Benefits.gov?

- The official benefits website of the U.S. government
- A tool to inform citizens of benefits for which they may be eligible
- A source providing information on how to apply for assistance
- A way to learn about FREE MONEY and GRANTS

You can browse benefits by state, category, federal agency, or other resources at http://www.benefits.gov/.

TAX CREDITS FOR HIGHER EDUCATION EXPENSES

Two tax credits help offset the costs (tuition, fees, books, supplies, equipment) of college or career school by reducing the amount of your income tax:

- The American Opportunity Credit allows you to claim up to $2,500 per student per year for the first four years of school as the student works toward a degree or similar credential.

- The Lifetime Learning Credit allows you to claim up to $2,000 per student per year for any college or career school tuition and fees, as well as for books, supplies, and equipment that were required for the course and had to be purchased from the school.

Even if you normally would not file a tax return because of your income level, be sure to do so. If you do not file, you will miss tax credits that put money in your pocket. Visit http://studentaid.ed.gov/types/tax-benefits for more information.

WATCH OUT: SCAMMERS TARGET JOB SEEKERS

- Beware of Online Job Classifieds Used to Steal Your Identity
  FINRA describes the latest variation of the identity theft tale. Stock traders, posing as employees of a made-up Latvian brokerage firm, appear to have stolen personal information from individuals who thought they were applying for a job through the popular classifieds website Craigslist.

- Look for Seven Red Flags when Searching for Jobs Online
  People are increasingly turning to the Internet as a key tool. In 2007, 73 percent of job seekers reported using the online sources compared to 66 percent in 2005. While the Internet has made searching for jobs easier it also provides an opportunity for ID thieves and scammers to take advantage of eager ~ and unsuspecting ~ job seekers.

- Scammers Target Job Hunters in Weak Economy
  As the unemployment rate hovers around 10 percent, the Better Business Bureau warns that scammers are taking advantage of the opportunity by preying on the unemployed. Identifying the common red flags of a fraud is one way for job hunters to protect themselves and their wallets.

WORK FROM HOME AND OTHER JOB SCAMS

- BBB Warns Against Twitter Money-Making Schemes
  Through Tweets, e-mails, and websites, job hunters are told they can make lots of money from the comfort of home using Twitter. The Better Business Bureau warns that the large print for such offers may promise participants big returns, but the fine print can cost them every month.

- BBB Warns Job Hunters to Steer Clear of Rebate Processing Job Scams
  Better Business Bureau is warning job hunters to beware of opportunities to work from home processing rebates. While the job offer may claim that people can earn up to a thousand dollars a day without leaving the comfort of home, the BBB has received hundreds of complaints from victims nationwide who never earned a dime and were, in fact, ripped off for hundreds of dollars in upfront fees.

- BBB Warns of Craigslist Job Scam
  A bogus employment opportunity fraud has surfaced on Craigslist claiming to offer a job with the Better Business Bureau. Scammers are

posting fake advertisements for employment opportunities for a Data Entry Clerk at the Better Business Bureau in regions across North America.

- Do Not Get Taken by a Modeling Scam
Whether you are interested in a modeling career, just want to make a few extra bucks, or you think your child might have a future in acting or modeling, be on the lookout for scammers. The Better Business Bureau warns that some modeling agencies are just trying to make a fast buck and do not deliver on promises of fame and fortune. In the last three years would-be models have researched agencies with the BBB more than half a million times. Unfortunately, the BBB also received more than 2,000 complaints from people who feel they were misled by an agency into paying large upfront fees — often for headshots and portfolios — and received little or no modeling or acting work in return.

- Enigma for Consumers: Mystery Shopping Jobs
An operation that told consumers they could be hired as mystery shoppers and earn a substantial income — and the telemarketing firm working for them — are facing Federal Trade Commission charges that their claims about job availability and income potential were deceptive.

- How I Got Taken by a Work-at-Home Scam
Work-at-home-scams are on the rise, consumer watchdog groups say. Scammers are busier than ever because tough economic times are making people more desperate to make money.

- Bogus Post Office Job Offers from Classified Ads
The Federal Trade Commission has charged an employment-opportunity scammer and his companies with marketing a fraudulent U.S. Postal Service (USPS) employment program. Through advertisements and telephone pitches, the defendants misrepresented that they were connected with or endorsed by USPS; that postal jobs were available; that customers would receive study materials to help them pass the postal entrance exam; and that customers who pass that exam were assured jobs with USPS. In reality, none of these claims are true.

TIPS FOR CHOOSING INSURANCE POLICIES

General sources of insurance information include the American Council of Life Insurers, the Insurance Information Institute, the National Association of

Insurance Commissioners, and your state insurance department. You can also visit insure.com.

When buying insurance, whether it is home, life, auto, rental, or other:

- Find out whether your state insurance department offers any information concerning insurance companies and rates. This is a good way to get a feeling for the range of prices and the lowest-cost providers in your area.

- Check several sources for the best deal. Try getting quotes from an insurance-focused website, but be aware that many online services may provide prices for just a few companies. An independent insurance agent that works with several insurers in your local area might be able to get you a better deal.

- Make sure the insurance company is licensed and covered by the state's guaranty fund. The fund pays claims in case the company defaults. Your state insurance department can provide this information.

- Check the financial stability and soundness of the insurance company. Ratings from A.M. Best, Standard and Poor's, and Moody's Investors Services are available online and at most public libraries.

- Research the complaint record of the company. Contact your state insurance department or visit the website of the National Association of Insurance Commissioners, which has a database of complaints filed with state regulators.

- Find out what others think about the company's customer service. Consumers can rate homeowner insurance companies at J.D. Power's website.

- Once you pay your first insurance premium make sure you receive a written policy. This tells you the agent forwarded your premium to the insurance company. If you do not receive a policy within 60 days, contact your agent and the insurance company.

If you suspect fraud call the National Insurance Crime Bureau's hotline at 1-800-835-6422. Alternatively, for more information, check out the Coalition Against Insurance Fraud website.

FAIRYDOGPARENTS.ORG

If you are faced with the choice of surrendering your dog because of personal financial circumstances, you may qualify for assistance. Fairy DogParents is a 501c3 nonprofit organization that helps prevent dogs from being surrendered to shelters. They provide assistance with food, medical, and general wellness needs of qualified dog recipients in Massachusetts.

Visit http://www.fairydogparents.org for more information.

Watch FairyDogParents.org as a CNN Hero at: http://www.cnn.com/2012/09/06/us/cnnheroes-manning-fairy-dogparents/index.html?iref=allsearch.

APPENDIX 2 — RESOURCE SHORT LIST

ADA.gov — Gateway to information about the Americans with Disabilities Act (ADA). The ADA gives civil rights protections to individuals with disabilities similar to those provided to individuals based on race, color, sex, national origin, age, and religion. Learn more about the ADA and other disability rights laws.

AIDS.gov — An information source to guide users to federal HIV/AIDS information and resources on topics including prevention, testing and treatment, and research programs.

AgingStats.gov — A website of the Federal Interagency Forum on Aging-Related Statistics.

Benefits.gov — Federal government website with detailed information on government benefit programs.

BullyingInfo.org — Offers resources on bullying, including a question and answer section, articles on cyber and electronic bullying, and ways to get involved in bullying prevention.

BuyAccessible.gov — Helps electronic and information technology (EIT) sellers and buyers meet the accessibility requirements of Section 508. Registered users of this site can find out if their products need to be 508-compliant and buyers can find sellers of 508-compliant products and services.

Could I Have LUPUS.gov — A federal website dedicated to the autoimmune disease that primarily affects women between ages 15 and 45. Each year more than 16,000 Americans develop this condition, which can affect various parts of the body, including the skin, joints, heart, lungs, blood, kidneys, and brain. Learn about lupus, its symptoms, treatment options, and available resources.

CuidadodeSalud.gov — Connects consumers to new information and resources to help them access quality, affordable healthcare coverage. CuidadodeSalud.gov is a partner site of HealthCare.gov and has information specifically for people with disabilities in the Personas con Incapacidad section of the site.

Data.ed.gov — Provides information about the U.S. Department of Education's activities, including the decision-making process, activities funded, and achievements. The site also includes a link to a pilot project on grant making.

Data.gov — Provides access to government information through downloadable apps and new Web technology. Users can locate information on everything from local crime statistics to environmental health to job statistics by town.

Digital Literacy Resources — Offers information on using a computer or mobile device, software, and applications to help build digital literacy skills.

DisasterAssistance.gov — This website is the result of Executive Order 13411, which requires the government to simplify the process of identifying and applying for disaster assistance. The site includes information about more than 40 kinds of disaster assistance. You can apply for assistance with a single online application.

E-Gov — Home page of the E-Gov initiative, using Internet-based technology, streamlining citizen-to-government communications.

EyeNote.gov — Provides an application developed by the Bureau of Engraving and Printing for the blind or visually impaired to use as a tool to increase accessibility to U.S. paper currency. It is built for the Apple iOS to allow the user to scan a bank note and communicate its value back to the user. The app is available as a free download on the Apple App Store.

FedStats.gov — Gateway to statistics from more than 100 U.S. federal agencies.

Fedshirevets.gov — Information gateway to federal employment for Veterans, transitioning service members, their families, federal human resource professionals, and hiring managers.

FindYouthInfo.gov —This website was created by the Interagency Working Group on Youth Programs (IWGYP), which is composed of representatives from 12 federal agencies that support programs and services focusing on youth. The IWGYP promotes the goal of positive, healthy outcomes for youth, including youth in transition. Check out the Map My Community tool to locate federally supported youth programs in your community.

Frequently Asked Questions (FAQs) of the U.S. Government — A list of FAQs from federal websites.

GovLoans.gov — Centralized source for federal loan information.

Grants.gov — Allows organizations to electronically find and apply for competitive grant opportunities from all federal grant-making agencies.

Health.gov — A portal to the websites of a number of multi-agency health initiatives and activities of the U.S. Department of Health and Human Services (HHS) and other federal departments and agencies.

HealthCare.gov — Find information about the Affordable Care Act and learn about insurance options, preventive services to keep you healthy, and how health coverage is being made more affordable for people with disabilities and others.

HealthyPeople.gov — A set of health objectives to improve the overall health of the nation in the next ten years. These objectives are meant to help a wide range of people with the goals to increase the quality and length of life and to remove the current health disparities that exist among specific segments within the population.

Kids.gov — Find links to government and other websites just for kids.

LetsMove.gov — Let's Move! is a comprehensive initiative launched by First Lady Michelle Obama to help combat childhood obesity. Families, schools, and communities can take action by learning the facts about obesity, how to eat healthier, being physically active every day, and joining a national call for community-based efforts to raise healthier children.

Making Home Affordable — Website provides information and assistance for America's homeowners, including self-assessment tools to help homeowners find out if they can benefit from refinancing or mortgage modification programs.

MedlinePlus — A website by the U.S. National Library of Medicine for patients and families that provides information about diseases, illnesses, health conditions, and wellness issues. Pages contain links with health information on over 800 topics, as well as information on drugs and supplements, videos, and tools.

My Skills My Future — Helps laid-off workers and other people who are changing careers find new occupations by identifying jobs that match skills and knowledge similar to their current or previous jobs. Users can also find local training programs and apply for jobs online.

MyMoney.gov — Website dedicated to teaching all Americans the basics of financial education. Whether you are buying a home, balancing your checkbook, or investing in your 401(k), the resources on MyMoney.gov can help you maximize your financial decisions.

National Contact Center — Provides answers to your questions about all federal programs, benefits, or services.

National Park Service — Gateway to information from the National Park Service on national parks including trails, vistas, camping, and accessible opportunities for people with disabilities.

National Resource Directory — Provides access to thousands of services and resources to help wounded warriors, Service Members, Veterans, and their families who support them.

OPPORTUNITY.gov — Information portal from the U.S. Departments of Education and Labor on educational opportunities and financial assistance to help unemployed workers find education and training to increase their job prospects.

Office of the Federal Register — Provides online search of public, federal government documents that include filings, rules, notices, federal laws, resolutions, presidential documents, federal programs, and activities.

Open Innovation Portal — U.S. Department of Education's website that provides a collaborative online community where members can identify, improve, and implement innovative solutions to educational challenges.

President's Committee for People with Intellectual Disabilities (PCPID) — PCPID works to expand educational opportunities, increase access to technology, improve individual and family support, increase employment and economic independence, and promote access and integration into community life for people with intellectual disabilities.

Ready.gov — Information from the U.S. Department of Homeland Security on how to be prepared in case of a national emergency, including a possible terrorist attack. Includes information relevant to businesses, employees, families, individuals with disabilities, and others.

Recreation.gov — Find answers to frequently asked questions about recreation, locate recreation areas in your state, make reservations for camp sites, and get information on camping, hiking, and other activities using the federal government's one-stop recreation website.

Reginfo.gov — Search and view information on current and historical data (as far back as the 1970s) from collective information reviews by the Office of Information and Regulatory Affairs. Federal agencies must submit information electronically to be tracked and is available to the public on this site.

Regulations.gov — Find, review, and submit comments on federal documents that are open for comment and published in the Federal Register, the government's legal newspaper.

STOPMedicareFraud.gov — U.S. Departments of Justice and Health and Human Services website that provides information on how to prevent fraud and abuse of the Medicare program. Includes tools such as the Senior Medicare Patrol Program to help older adults volunteer in the fight against Medicare fraud.

Section508.gov — Clearinghouse of information on Section 508 of the Rehabilitation Act, which requires federal agencies to make their electronic and information technology accessible to people with disabilities.

Serve.gov — Program administered by the Corporation for National and Community Service that provides information about volunteer opportunities in your community.

StopFraud.gov — Maintains a comprehensive list of resources and information dedicated to helping find and report suspected cases of financial fraud.

Student Aid on the Web — Find free information from the U.S. Department of Education on preparing for and funding education beyond high school.

Students.gov — Information geared toward teens including community service options, how to pay for college, information about military service, and how to register to vote.

Telework.Gov — The U.S. Office of Personnel Management and the U.S. General Services Administration established this interagency website to easily access information on telework in federal agencies. Find information on federal telework policies and guidelines, frequently asked questions, and whom to contact about procedures and guidelines in specific federal agencies.

USA.gov — Gateway to U.S. government information, services, and resources.

USAJOBS.gov — Gateway to federal government jobs and employment information.

White House Disabilities Web Page — Learn about the Obama Administration's priorities and initiatives as they relate to increasing the employment, community integration, and independence of Americans with disabilities. http://www.whitehouse.gov/issues/disabilities

BIBLIOGRAPHY

"17 Ways to Reinvent Yourself While You Are Unemployed." *LinkedIn 101*. N.p., n.d. Web. 24 Sept. 2012. <http://linkedin101.wordpress.com/2010/11/02/17-ways-to-reinvent-yourself-while-youre-unemployed/>.

"5 Stages of Grieving Over a Job Loss." *5 Stages of Grieving Over a Job Loss*. N.p., n.d. Web. 24 Sept. 2012. <http://www.cluewagon.com/2009/03/5-stages-of-grieving-over-a-job-loss/>.

"8 Things Unemployed People Can Do That Look Good on a Resume." *Free Online Resume Builder*. Yellow Brick Road.com, n.d. Web. 20 Aug.2012. <http://www.yellowbrickroad.com/follow/8-things-unemployed-people-look-good-resume/>.

"About CareerOneStop." About CareerOneStop. U. S. Department of Labor, n.d. Web. 16 Sept. 2012. <http://www.careeronestop.org/COS_Aboutus.aspx>.

"About United Way Worldwide." United Way. United Way Worldwide, n.d. Web. 13 Sept. 2012. <http://www.unitedway.org/pages/about-united-way-worldwide/>.

"About Us.": Disability.gov. U.S. Government, n.d. Web. 14 Sept. 2012. <https://www.disability.gov/home/about_us>.

"Accountability Partners | CEO Peer Groups | Executive Coaching | Technology Peer Group | Sales Consultants Chicago | Executive Development." *Accountability Partners | CEO Peer Groups | Executive Coaching | Technology Peer Group | Sales Consultants Chicago | Executive Development*. N.p., n.d. Web. 24 Sept. 2012. <http://accountabilitypartners.com/index.html>.

"Advice for the Long-Term Unemployed." *Advice for the Long-Term Unemployed*. Martynemko.com, n.d. Web. 21 Aug. 2012. <http://www.martynemko.com/articles/advice-for-long-term-unemployed_id1263>.

"Avoiding Scams." Home. U.S. Department of Education, n.d. Web. 25 Aug. 2012. <http://studentaid.ed.gov/types/scams>.

"Benefits.gov - Federal Employee Dental and Vision Insurance Program (FEDVIP)." Benefits.gov - Federal Employee Dental and Vision Insurance Program (FEDVIP). U.S. Office of Personnel Management, n.d. Web. 17 Sept. 2012. <http://www.benefits.gov/benefits/benefit-details/4587>.

"Benefits.gov - Loan/Loan Repayment." Benefits.gov - Loan/Loan Repayment. U.S. Government, n.d. Web. 11 Sept. 2012. <http://www.benefits.gov/benefits/browse-by-category/category/LOA%20>.

"Blog." *5 Things to Do When You are Unemployed. Hint: It's Not Job Hunting.* N.p., n.d. Web. 24 Sept. 2012. <http://blog.penelopetrunk.com/2009/03/06/5-things-to-do-when-youre-unemployed-hint-its-not-job-hunting/>.

"Career Counseling." *- Unemployed.* N.p., n.d. Web. 24 Sept. 2012. <http://www.unemployment911.com/career-counseling.htm>.

"Center for Women Veterans: About Us - Center for Women Veterans." Center for Women Veterans: About Us - Center for Women Veterans. U.S. Department of Veterans Affairs, 18 Jan. 2012. Web. 16 Sept. 2012. <http://www.va.gov/WOMENVET/about.asp>.

"Credit - General Tips | USA.gov." Credit - General Tips | USA.gov. U.S. Government, 20 Aug. 2012. Web. 22 Aug. 2012. <http://www.usa.gov/topics/money/credit/tips.shtml>.

"Credit - Protect Your Credit | USA.gov." Credit - Protect Your Credit | USA. gov. U.S. Government, 20 Aug. 2012. Web. 22 Aug. 2012. <http://www.usa.gov/topics/consumer/scams-fraud/credit-card.shtml>.

"Did You Know That the Internal Revenue Service (IRS) Provides Tax Benefits for Education?" Tax Benefits. U.S. Department of Education, n.d. Web. 11 Sept. 2012. <http://studentaid.ed.gov/types/tax-benefits>.

"Email to a Friend." *Cover Letter Sample for an Unemployed Job Seeker.* Monster.com, n.d. Web. 20 Aug. 2012. <http://career-advice.monster.com/resumes-cover-letters/cover-letter-samples/sample-cover-letter-unemployed/article.aspx>.

"Email to a Friend." *Interview Questions (and Answers) for the Unemployed.* Monster.com, n.d. Web. 21 Aug. 2012. <http://career-advice.monster.ca/job-interview/interview-questions/interview-questions-when-unemployed-canada/article.aspx>.

"Expanded Food and Nutrition Education Program (EFNEP)." Expanded Food and Nutrition Education Program (EFNEP). U.S. Department of Agriculture, 17 May 2012. Web. 16 Sept. 2012. <http://www.csrees.usda.gov/nea/food/efnep/efnep.html>.

"Facebook Partners with U.S. Labor Department to Help Unemployed." *Digital Trends.* N.p., n.d. Web. 24 Sept. 2012. <http://www.digitaltrends.com/social-media/facebook-partners-with-u-s-labor-department-to-help-unemployed/>.

"Fact Sheet on the Legal Services Corporation." LSC. Legal Services Corporation, n.d. Web. 13 Sept. 2012. <http://lsc.gov/about/what-is-lsc>.

"Fact Sheet: President Obama Announces New Steps to Provide Housing Relief to Veterans and Servicemembers and Help More Responsible Homeowners Refinance." The White House. The White House, 6 Mar. 2012. Web. 14 Aug. 2012. <http://www.whitehouse.gov/the-press-office/2012/03/06/fact-sheet-president-obama-announces-new-steps-provide-housing-relief-ve>.

"Federal Student Loans for College or Career School Are an Investment in Your Future." Loans. U.S. Department of Education, n.d. Web. 11 Sept. 2012. <http://studentaid.ed.gov/types/loans>.

"Federal Trade Commission Protecting America's Consumers." FTC Bureau of Consumer Protection. Federal Trade Commission, 14 Apr. 2010. Web. 22 Aug. 2012. <http://www.ftc.gov/bcp/menus/consumer/credit.shtm>.

"Federal Trade Commission Protecting America's Consumers." FTC Consumer Information. Federal Trade Commission, 13 Mar. 2003. Web. 13 Sept. 2012. <http://www.ftc.gov/bcp/menus/consumer/credit/rights.shtm>.

"Federal Trade Commission Protecting America's Consumers." Knee Deep in Debt. Federal Trade Commission, 23 Apr. 2012. Web. 13 Sept. 2012. <http://www.ftc.gov/bcp/edu/pubs/consumer/credit/cre19.shtm>.

"Finding Low-Cost Dental Care." Finding Low-Cost Dental Care. National Institute of Dental and Craniofacial Research, Nov. 2011. Web. 17 Sept. 2012. <http://www.nidcr.nih.gov/OralHealth/PopularPublications/FindingLowCostDentalCare/>.

"Food, Nutrition, and Fitness | USA.gov." Food, Nutrition, and Fitness | USA.gov. U.S. Government, 20 Aug. 2012. Web. 22 Aug. 2012. <http://www.usa.gov/Citizen/Topics/Health/Food.shtml>.

"Foreclosure Resources | USA.gov." Foreclosure Resources | USA.gov. U.S. Government, 8 Aug. 2012. Web. 14 Aug. 2012. <http://www.usa.gov/Citizen/Topics/Family/Homeowners/Foreclosure.shtml>.

"Get a Job." Why You Should Network -. N.p., n.d. Web. 24 Sept. 2012. <http://www.netplaces.com/job-search/networking/why-you-should-network.htm>.

"Goodwill for You." Goodwill Industries International. Goodwill Industries International, 2012. Web. 25 Oct. 2012. <http://www.goodwill.org/goodwill-for-you/>.

"Government Benefits, Grants, and Financial Aid for Citizens | USA.gov." Government Benefits, Grants, and Financial Aid for Citizens | USA.gov. U.S. Government, 8 Aug. 2012. Web. 17 Aug. 2012. <http://www.usa.gov/Citizen/Topics/Benefits.shtml>.

"Grants.gov - Home." Grants.gov - Home. U.S. Department of Health and Human Services, n.d. Web. 17 Aug. 2012. <http://www.grants.gov/>.

"Health Insurance | USA.gov." Health Insurance | USA.gov. U.S. Government, 20 Aug. 2012. Web. 04 Sept. 2012. <http://www.usa.gov/Citizen/Topics/Health/HealthInsurance.shtml>.

"Home - English | MyMoney." Home - English | MyMoney. U.S. Government, 25 July 2012. Web. 25 Aug. 2012. <http://www.mymoney.gov/index.html>.

"Home Improvements/U.S. Department of Housing and Urban Development (HUD)." Home Improvements/U.S. Department of Housing and Urban Development (HUD). U.S. Department of Housing and Urban Development, n.d. Web. 22 Aug. 2012. <http://portal.hud.gov/hudportal/HUD?src=/topics/home_improvements>.

"How to Get Counseling While Unemployed October 20, 2010 8:58 AM A Subscribe." *How to Get Counseling While Unemployed?* N.p., n.d. Web. 24 Sept. 2012. <http://ask.metafilter.com/168270/How-to-get-counseling-while-unemployed>.

"Jobs and Education Scams | USA.gov." Jobs and Education Scams | USA.gov. U.S. Government, 8 Aug. 2012. Web. 17 Aug. 2012. <http://www.usa.gov/topics/consumer/scams-fraud/jobs-education/index.shtml>.

"Making Home Affordable An Official Program of the Departments of the Treasury & Housing and Urban Development." View All Programs. Make Home Affordable, 15 June 2012. Web. 14 Aug. 2012. <http://www.makinghomeaffordable.gov/programs/view-all-programs/Pages/default.aspx>.

"Mortgages for Home Buyers and Homeowners | USA.gov." Mortgages for Home Buyers and Homeowners | USA.gov. U.S. Government, 8 Aug. 2012. Web. 14 Aug. 2012. <http://www.usa.gov/shopping/realestate/mortgages/mortgages.shtml>.

"Negotiating." *About.com Career Planning.* N.p., n.d. Web. 24 Sept. 2012. <http://careerplanning.about.com/od/negotiatingoffers/Negotiating.htm>.

"Newsroom." Benefits.gov. U.S. Government, n.d. Web. 25 Aug. 2012. <http://www.benefits.gov/>.

"Other Resources." Disability.gov. U.S. Government, nod Web. 14 Sept. 2012. <https://www.disability.gov/home/other_resources>.

"Rapid Response Services For Laid Off Workers." Rapid Response Services For Laid Off Workers. U.S. Department of Labor |, 5 Sept. 2012. Web. 16 Sept. 2012.

<http://www.doleta.gov/layoff/workers.cfm>.

"Replacing Your Vital Documents | USA.gov." Replacing Your Vital Documents | USA.gov. U.S. Government, 20 Aug. 2012. Web. 13 Sept. 2012. <http://www.usa.gov/Citizen/Topics/Family-Issues/Vital-Docs.shtml>.

"Returning Service Members (OEF/OIF) Home." Returning Service Members (OEF/OIF) Home. U.S. Department of Veterans Affairs, 2 Aug. 2012. Web. 16 Sept. 2012. <http://www.oefoif.va.gov/>.

"Safety at Home." The Why and How of Water Conservation. UL, LLC, n.d. Web. 21 Aug. 2012. <http://www.safetyathome.com/environmental-safety/environmental-safety-articles/the-why-and-how-of-water-conservation/?gclid=CLzT79LJ-bECFQs3nAodQhgAGA>.

"SBA Direct." Small Business Loans. U.S. Small Business Administration, n.d. Web. 25 Aug. 2012. <http://www.sba.gov/category/navigation-structure/loans-grants/small-business-loans>.

"SBA Direct: Find What Matters Most to You…" Procurement Technical Assistance Centers (PTACs). U.S. Small Business Administration, n.d. Web. 27 Sept. 2012. <http://www.sba.gov/content/procurement-technical-assistance-centers-ptacs>.

"SBA Direct: Find What Matters Most to You…" SCORE. U.S. Small Business Administration, n.d. Web. 27 Sept. 2012. <http://www.sba.gov/content/score>.

"SBA Direct: Find What Matters Most to You…" Small Business Development Centers (SBDCs). U.S. Small Business Administration, n.d. Web. 27 Sept. 2012. <http://www.sba.gov/content/small-business-development-centers-sbdcs>.

"SBA Direct: Find What Matters Most to You…" Veterans Business Outreach Centers. U.S. Small Business Administration, n.d. Web. 27 Sept. 2012. <http://www.sba.gov/content/veterans-business-outreach-centers>.

"SBA Direct: Find What Matters Most to You…" Women's Business Centers. U.S.Small Business Administration, n.d. Web. 27 Sept. 2012. <http://www.sba.gov/content/womens-business-centers>.

"Senior Citizens' Resources | USA.gov." Senior Citizens' Resources | USA.gov. U.S. Government, 20 Aug. 2012. Web. 22 Aug. 2012. <http://www.usa.gov/Topics/Seniors.shtml>.

"Serve.gov | About Serve.gov." Serve.gov | About Serve.gov. Corporation for National and Community Service, 24 May 2010. Web. 13 Sept. 2012. <http://www.serve.gov/about.asp>.

"Talk to a Housing Counselor/U.S. Department of Housing and Urban Development (HUD)." Talk to a Housing Counselor/U.S. Department of Housing and Urban Development (HUD). HUD, n.d. Web. 14 Aug. 2012. <http://portal.hud.gov/hudportal/HUD?src=/i_want_to/talk_to_a_housing_counselor>.

"Tips for Choosing an Insurance Policy | USA.gov." Tips for Choosing an Insurance Policy | USA.gov. U.S. Government, 20 Aug. 2012. Web. 23 Aug. 2012. <http://www.usa.gov/topics/money/insurance/tips.shtml>.

"Training." U.S. Department of Labor. U.S. Department of Labor, n.d. Web. 15 Aug. 2012. <http://www.dol.gov/dol/topic/training/index.htm>.

"U.S. Export Assistance Centers | SBA.gov." U.S. Export Assistance Centers | SBA.gov. U.S. Small Business Administration, n.d. Web. 27 Sept. 2012. <http://www.sba.gov/content/us-export-assistance-centers>.

"Understanding Your Medical Bills." American Academy of Family Physicians, 1 Jan. 2012. Web. 16 Sept. 2012. <http://familydoctor.org/familydoctor/en/healthcare-management/insurance-bills/understanding-your-medical-bills.html>.

"Unemployed? Here Are Five Bad Social Media Habits to Quit ASAP." *LockerGnome.* N.p., n.d. Web. 24 Sept. 2012. <http://www.lockergnome.com/social/2011/11/29/unemployed-here-are-five-bad-social-media-habits-to-quit-asap/>.

"USA.gov: * Help for the Unemployed: Apply for Unemployment Benefits." USA.gov: * Help for the Unemployed: Apply for Unemployment Benefits. U.S. Government, n.d. Web. 22 Aug. 2012. <http://1.usa.gov/nNQQuj>.

"USA.gov: * Housing Assistance: Housing Choice Voucher Program." USA.gov: * Housing Assistance: Housing Choice Voucher Program. U.S. Government, 31 Aug. 2012. Web. 14 Aug. 2012. <http://1.usa.gov/rqJ2qs>.

"USA.gov: * Housing Assistance: Rent Payments." USA.gov: * Housing Assistance: Rent Payments. U.S. Government, 31 Aug. 2012. Web. 14 Aug. 2012. <http://1.usa.gov/nxYFHd>.

"USA.gov: Assistance with Medical Bills." USA.gov: Assistance with Medical Bills. U.S. Government, 23 July 2012. Web. 16 Sept. 2012. <http://1.usa.gov/o8d7HF>.

"USA.gov: Help for the Homeless." USA.gov: Help for the Homeless. U.S. Government, 31 Aug. 2012. Web. 14 Aug. 2012. <http://1.usa.gov/njNByI>.

"USDA Rural Development-HSF-SFH." USDA Rural Development-HSF-SFH. U.S. Department of Agriculture, 20 Aug. 2012. Web. 22 Aug. 2012. <http://www.

rurdev.usda.gov/HSF_SFH.html>.

"Vocational Rehabilitation and Employment Service Home Page." Vocational Rehabilitation and Employment Service Home Page. U.S. Department of Veterans Affairs, 31 July 2012. Web. 22 Aug. 2012. <http://www.vba.va.gov/bln/vre/>.

"Volunteering in America." Volunteering in America. U.S. Government, 9 Aug. 2011. Web. 22 Aug. 2012. <http://www.volunteeringinamerica.gov/>.

"Ways to Reinvent Yourself." *SUCCESS Magazine.* N.p., n.d. Web. 24 Sept. 2012. <http://www.success.com/articles/1280-ways-to-reinvent-yourself>.

"What We Do | SBA.gov." What We Do | SBA.gov. U.S. Small Business Administration, n.d. Web. 27 Sept. 2012. <http://www.sba.gov/about-sba-services/what-we-do>.

"When It's Hot." EPA. Environmental Protection Agency, n.d. Web. 21 Aug. 2012. <http://www.epa.gov/watersense/our_water/when_its_hot.html>.

"Where to Write for Vital Records." Centers for Disease Control and Prevention. Centers for Disease Control and Prevention, 27 June 2012. Web. 21 Aug. 2012. <http://www.cdc.gov/nchs/w2w.htm>.

"Who We Serve." Goodwill Industries International. Goodwill Industries International, 2012. Web. 25 Oct. 2012. <http://www.goodwill.org/goodwill-for-you/specialized-services/>.

"Employment Termination Checklist." Worm Law Firm, P.C.

America, Scholarship. "Compare 5 Top Scholarship Search Engines." US News. U.S.News & World Report, 20 Jan. 2011. Web. 11 Sept. 2012. <http://www.usnews.com/education/blogs/the-scholarship-coach/2011/01/20/compare-5-top-scholarship-search-engines>.

Beesley, Caron. "Small Business Lending Is Improving: Tips for Finding and Securing the Right Loan | SBA.gov." Small Business Lending Is Improving: Tips for Finding and Securing the Right Loan | SBA.gov. U.S. Small Business Administration, 11 June 2012. Web. 06 Sept. 2012. <http://www.sba.gov/community/blogs/small-business-lending-improving-tips-finding-and-securing-right-loan>.

Beesley, Caron. "Starting a Business? 10 Steps Every Entrepreneur Needs to Know | SBA.gov." Starting a Business? 10 Steps Every Entrepreneur Needs to Know | SBA.gov. U.S. Small Business Administration, 21 May 2012. Web. 06 Sept. 2012. <http://www.sba.gov/community/blogs/starting-business-10-steps-every-

entrepreneur-needs-know>.

Career Advice & News Center." *Debunking 5 (Un)employment Myths*. N.p., n.d. Web. 24 Sept. 2012. <http://www.job.com/career-advice/job-search-advice/debunking-5-unemployment-myths.html>.

Delaney, Arthur. "Bridge To Work: Obama's Plan For Long-Term Unemployed." *The Huffington Post*. TheHuffingtonPost.com, 08 Sept. 2011. Web. 24 Sept. 2012. <http://www.huffingtonpost.com/2011/09/08/obama-jobs-plan-bridge-to-work-program-long-term-unemployed_n_953838.html>.

Donahue, Theresa. "25 Excellent College Scholarship Search Engines Online University Data." Online University Data. Online University Data, 3 June 2010. Web. 11 Sept. 2012. <http://onlineuniversitydata.com/2010/25-excellent-college-scholarship-search-engines/>.?

Horn, Carl Van, and The Opinions Expressed in This Commentary Are Solely Those of Carl Van Horn. "5 Myths about Unemployment Insurance - CNN.com." CNN. Cable News Network, 02 Dec. 2011. Web. 24 Sept. 2012. <http://www.cnn.com/2011/12/02/opinion/van-horn-unemployment-extension/index.html>.

How to Cope When Coworkers Lose Their Jobs." *About.com Human Resources*. N.p., n.d. Web. 24 Sept. 2012. <http://humanresources.about.com/od/layoffsdownsizing/a/survivors_cope.htm>.

Kavoussi, Bonnie. "'Career Gear,' 'Dress For Success' Give Suits To Unemployed For Job Interviews." *The Huffington Post*. TheHuffingtonPost.com, 11 July 2012. Web. 24 Sept. 2012. <http://www.huffingtonpost.com/2012/07/11/career-gear-dress-for-success-suitsunemployed_n_1664506.html>.

Negotiate Your Severance Package. Forbes Magazine, n.d. Web. 21 Aug. 2012. <http://negotiateseverance.com/>.

Nutter, Ron. "20 Ways to Survive a Layoff." Network World. Network World, Inc., 25 Aug. 2008. Web. 08 Sept. 2012. <http://www.networkworld.com/news/2008/082508-job-tips.html?page=1>.

Rosenberg McKay, Dawn. "Five Things Not to Do When You Leave Your Job." About.com Career Planning. About.com, n.d. Web. 08 Sept. 2012. <http://careerplanning.about.com/od/jobseparation/a/leave_mistakes.htm>.

Saving to Invest. Saving to Invest.com, n.d. Web. 21 Aug. 2012. <http://www.savingtoinvest.com/2010/12/being-laid-off-negotiate-that-severance-package.html>.

Taylor, Philip. "52 Ways to Make Extra Money." How to Make Extra Money. PT Money, 16 May 2012. Web. 14 Aug. 2012. <http://ptmoney.com/52-ways-make-extra-money/>.

The Trade Adjustment Assistance Program. N.p.: n.p., n.d. U.S. Department of Labor. Web. <http://www.doleta.gov/tradeact/pdf/2011_brochure.pdf>.

Time for a Career Assessment? Monster.com, n.d. Web. 21 Aug. 2012. <http://career-advice.monster.com/job-search/career-assessment/2010-career-assessment-and-change/article.aspx>.

Unemployed? 11 Options for Finding Work Today. Financial Highway.com, n.d. Web. 21 Aug. 2012. <http://financialhighway.com/unemployed-ten-options-for-finding-work-today/>.

Ways to Get Free Job Training. Bank Rate.com, n.d. Web. 21 Aug. 2012. <http://www.bankrate.com/finance/personal-finance/5-ways-to-get-free-job-training-1.aspx>.

Woods, Gae-Lynn. "Why Is It Important to Do Volunteer Work?" LIVESTRONG. COM. Demand Media, Inc., 30 Mar. 2011. Web. 13 Sept. 2012. <http://www.livestrong.com/article/190888-why-is-it-important-to-do-volunteer-work/>.

NICOLE ANTOINETTE

Nicole Antoinette has experienced a layoff three times in her 20-year career as an information technology professional. She is an author, independent Business Consultant, Adjunct College Professor, and owner of Faith Books & MORE Publishing.

After leading large teams in corporate America for 17 years, Nicole launched Faith Books & MORE in June 2008 by faith as promised in her life verse: "I will instruct you and teach you in the way you should go; I will counsel you and watch over you" (Psalm 32:8). She believes writers have an obligation to preserve their thoughts, experiences, creativity, and most importantly, their faith in print as well as other forms of media.

Nicole is a results-driven Information Technology Professional with multi-faceted technology experience leading large implementation engagements. She has experience working directly with and presenting to C-level executive leadership with strong leadership qualifications in management and planning, developing processes, building high-performance teams, and managing innovation. Nicole is recognized as a perceptive leader with demonstrated ability to lead a diverse team of professionals. She has twenty years of experience in Executive Leadership, Process Improvement, Project Management, Program Management, Software Quality Assurance, and Business Analysis with in-depth working knowledge and hands-on experience in Software Development Life Cycle, Software Quality Assurance methodologies and tools, managing SaaS, Clouding Computing, and eCommerce projects.

Nicole earned her Master of Science degree in Computer Information Systems from Missouri State University and her Bachelor of Business Administration degree (with majors in both Management Information Systems and Marketing) while playing basketball on a scholarship at Ohio University.

Nicole is a member of Free Chapel in Gainesville, GA. She currently resides in Suwanee, GA. Her son is an aspiring film director studying at the University of Southern California in the School of Cinematic Arts.

● ● ● ● ● ● ● ● ● ● ● ● ● ● ● ●

JILL COX-CORDOVA

Jill Cox-Cordova is a job layoff survivor and former hiring manager.

She has spent her entire career trying to affect change with her writing, her journalistic expertise, and her Write Avenue business.

She has worked as a professor and as a journalist for many television, print, and online media organizations nationwide, including NBC, MSNBC, The Weather Channel, CNN, and Essence magazine. Now a certified professional resume writer, she helps mid-level career professionals who are in transition by coaching and conducting career-enhancing webinars.

Jill graduated from Macalester College in St. Paul, MN, where she majored in International Studies and journalism. She earned her master's in Broadcast Journalism from the Medill School of Journalism at Northwestern University.

She resides with her husband, Anthony, in Kennesaw, Georgia, where they attend Thankful Baptist Church.

BOOKS BY NICOLE ANTOINETTE

BOX OF CHOCOLATES
ISBN: 978-0-9860247-5-7

BOX OF CHOCOLATES FOR TEENS
ISBN: 978-0-9860247-6-4

BUILDING BLOCKS FOR EFFECTIVE SOFTWARE TESTING
ISBN: 978-0-9820197-1-9

HOW TO MARKET YOUR BOOK FOR FREE: 2010 EDITION
ISBN: 978-0-9860159-7-7

STRATEGIC LIFE PLANNING FOR SINGLE PARENTS
ISBN: 978-0-9860247-9-5

THE EXECUTIVE'S GUIDE TO COST OPTIMIZATION
ISBN: 978-0-9820197-3-3

GETTING BEYOND THE DAY™ - YOUR GUIDE TO SURVIVING A JOB LAYOFF WORKBOOK
ISBN: 978-0-9860159-6-0

Fight another Fight to Dream another Dream

CPSIA information can be obtained at www.ICGtesting.com
Printed in the USA
LVOW081406301112

309531LV00006B/93/P